Impossible Theology

The Christian Evolutionist Dilemma

Mike Gascoigne

Anno Mundi Books

ISBN 0-9543922-1-3

Published by:
Anno Mundi Books
PO Box 752
Camberley
GU17 0XJ
England

Table of Contents

Table of Contents

Preface

In my first book, *Forgotten History of the Western People*, I showed that history is continuous, from the beginning of the world up to the present time, and drew attention to important accounts of the ancient world that have become largely forgotten as a consequence of evolution. These included creation and flood stories that come from non-Biblical cultures, together with stories from Greek mythology that bear a resemblance to the early descendants of Noah.

During the last few decades, Creation Science has accumulated many convincing proofs that the world in which we live must have been designed, and it cannot have come about by mere accident. This should inspire historians with new self-confidence, that they can pursue their investigations with total disregard for the suggestion made by some, that our earliest ancestors were ape-like hominids. Casting all this aside, we can examine the records passed down to us from antiquity, in the knowledge that however distorted and mythical some of these accounts might appear, they must have an underlying basis of fact.

Building upon this foundation, I attempted to revive the practice of writing histories that start from the beginning, and I call it "Creation History".

Forgotten History of the Western People was received with enthusiasm by those who believed in creation, as it is described in the Bible, because it supported their point of view. Most of these people were Christians of various theological persuasions, but the response from Christians as a whole was less certain. The problem was, even among Evangelicals who would have been staunchly creationist only a few years ago, there was uncertainty about where they stand on the issue. I felt that I was taking creation research one step further, supplementing science with history, while my companions in the church were going in the opposite direction, carrying around the baggage that this world calls "science" and never taking the time to find out what they were carrying.

1

I call it "baggage" because most people don't take the trouble to study creation and evolution in any great detail, and this includes the majority of Christians. They simply inherit the values of the society in which they live. We might be able to trust ourselves to the surgeon's knife because we believe that he has studied his science impartially, but we cannot trust the question of creation and evolution to experts in the same way. The debate has always been driven by philosophical ideologies, across the religious and secular divide, so that we can't trust anybody and we have to study the subject for ourselves.

Christians might be able to carry the baggage of evolution for a while, but they will have to throw it off sometime, otherwise it will weigh upon them heavily, causing them to preach a theology that is unsustainable. Not only do they have to rationalise the first three chapters of Genesis, but they also have to find compromise solutions for many other passages of Scripture. The biggest problem is the question of death before sin. If God created the world and saw that it was good, and if evolution is the mechanism that God used in his work of creation, then the millions of years of death and destruction that are required by evolution must also be good. In that case, what was the purpose of the resurrection of Jesus Christ from the dead? Why should he rise victorious, conquering death, if in fact death was something good?

This is just one of the many imponderables of the theological minefield that emerges when Christians take on board the baggage of evolution. Liberally-minded Christians have lived with these problems for years, and it doesn't seem to bother them much, but for Evangelicals it's more difficult. They have a high view of the Bible, proclaiming it as the "infallible Word of God", but they have to know how to answer people who say "Yes, but what does it mean?"

This book attempts to address these issues, not by making theological compromises, but by showing how the Gospel stands up if you believe in creation, and falls down if you believe in evolution. The scientific arguments are given in the Appendices, to help those who doubt, although basically it's a question of whether we believe the Word of God or not, and I hope that this book will help people to make up their minds.

I do not claim to have the last word on everything, and if there is more to be added to the material presented here, the discussion will continue on my website:

www.annomundi.co.uk

The main text of this book deals with two opposing theologies called the Real Gospel and the Pseudo-Gospel, followed by some practical considerations about the approach to theological study in churches and home-based groups.

The appendices, which take up as much space as the main text, are about philosophical and scientific issues. I have included these because it is necessary to show that there is scientific support for creationist theology. There are many other books that I could refer to on these issues, but I felt it was right to give my own interpretation of science, so that the issues are discussed right here, and the reader does not have to go and look at another book.

There is, in any case, a long tradition of matching up different disciplines such as science, philosophy, theology and history into a single holistic world-view. Probably one of the best examples is Isaac Newton who gave us the foundational principles of motion, gravity and the nature of light, and then he spent the rest of his life working on a Biblically based chronology of the ancient world.[1]

When quoting from the Bible, I have used the King James Authorised Version (KJAV)[2], except where specified. I do not consider it to be perfect, but I prefer to use it, in spite of its archaic language, because it is based on source documents that have been in common use for centuries. Many of the modern translations are based on manuscripts of greater antiquity which have survived intact, but only because they were not so commonly used, and this implies a lack of confidence in their reliability.

---

[1] Manuel, Frank, *Isaac Newton: Historian.*
[2] Extracts from the Authorised Version of the Bible (The King James Bible), the rights in which are vested in the Crown, are reproduced by permission of the Crown's Patentee, Cambridge University Press.

The seemingly antiquated language of the KJAV has one important advantage over modern text. It represents the source documents more accurately because it uses the singular personal pronouns *thee* and *thou*, and the plural *you*, maintaining a distinction that is present in both Hebrew and Greek.

I have made references to books, periodicals and Web pages where appropriate. Web pages tend to be transient, moving from one site to another, and sometimes disappearing altogether, but all the referenced pages were working in March 2004 when this book was being prepared for publication.

Acknowledgements

I would like to thank Helga Longworth, who has been regularly meeting with us for Bible study, and has given me some useful comments on theological issues, especially Bible prophecy. Also I would like to thank John Missenden, my fellow-student from the distant past at Leeds University, who has given me his comments on thermodynamics. But most of all I would like to thank my wife, Fiona, for proof reading the complete manuscript, and for her endless patience and support while I have been working on this book.

Chapter 1 - The Real Gospel

Back in the 1960's, I was a counsellor at the Billy Graham Crusade, held at Earls Court, London, although I wasn't at Earls Court itself. I was at a cinema in Stockton-on-Tees, where the meetings were being relayed using a projector linked to the telephone line.

Billy Graham would preach his sermon, and then he would come out with his usual phrase "I want you to get up out of your seat", and people would come forward for counselling.

They came forward for various reasons. There were people who had been Christians for a long time, but their love for the Lord had grown cold and they wanted to talk to someone. There were others who wanted to deal with specific problems that were hindering their spiritual life.

The largest group, probably about half of all those who responded, were people who had never believed in Jesus and wanted to receive salvation. For these people, we used a standard set of Bible verses as follows:

> For all have sinned, and come short of the glory of God. (Rom. 3:23)

> For the wages [penalty] of sin is death; but the gift of God is eternal life through Jesus Christ our Lord. (Rom. 6:23)

> But God commendeth his love toward us, in that, while we were yet sinners, Christ died for us. (Rom. 5:8)

> If we confess our sins, he is faithful and just to forgive us our sins, and to cleanse us from all unrighteousness. (1 John 1:9)

> For God so loved the world, that he gave his only begotten Son, that whosoever believeth in him should not perish, but have everlasting life. (John 3:16)

The reason we used these verses was because it was the simplest way of explaining to people, from the Bible, how to be saved. We could have explained it in our own words, but we used the Bible because we wanted people to see that the free gift of salvation was actually there, and we were not just giving our own opinions. In those days, the Bible could easily be used in that way because it was considered to have *authority*.

Even among non-Christians who never went to church, there was a sense of respect for the Bible. They understood that the Bible, for a long time, had been the bedrock of our society and the basis of laws and morals. Even if they had never read it for themselves, they were exposed to it at school assembly and possibly at church parade in the Scouts and Guides.

People understood about creation and the fall, and that we all have an eternal destiny of some sort, and they hoped that they would end up in a place called "heaven", but they had various misconceptions about how to get there. They thought they could get there by being good, and not doing too many things wrong, or by going to church, and the objective of the Billy Graham crusades and other types of Christian evangelism was to get this point straightened out.

We receive eternal life, not by any merit of our own, nor by any activities that we might undertake, but by the crucifixion and resurrection of Jesus Christ, and we simply have to respond to him.

Life and Death

It isn't so easy now, explaining to people the message of salvation in just a few Bible verses. They don't have the same respect for the Bible any more, and in particular they have difficulty with phrases like *"The penalty of sin is death"*. We all know we are going to die physically one day, and most people presuppose that the process of death and destruction has been going on for millions of years of evolution, and there is nothing unusual about it, so the death that comes as a consequence of sin must be limited to some kind of spiritual death. Indeed it was a spiritual death, when Adam and Eve committed their first sin, and were thrown out of the Garden of Eden. However, it also meant physical death, and we will soon get into this issue, but first we need to look at the creation itself, and how it was intended to be. On several occasions, God described his creation as being good.

- On the first day, when God created the heaven and the earth *"God saw the light, that it was good: and God divided the light from the darkness."* (Gen. 1:4).

- On the second day, there is no specific statement that what God made was good, but we will see how this is covered by the sixth day.

- On the third day, God divided the waters under the heaven (atmosphere) so that there was land and sea. *"... and God saw that it was good."* (Gen. 1:10). Then God continued his work on that day, creating vegetation. *"... and God saw that it was good."* (Gen. 1:12). So God declared his satisfaction with his work, twice on the same day.

- On the fourth day, God made the sun, moon and stars *"... and God saw that it was good."* (Gen. 1:18).

- On the fifth day, God created sea creatures and birds *"... and God saw that it was good. And God blessed them, saying, Be fruitful, and multiply, ..."* (Gen. 1:21-22).

- On the sixth day, God created animals that live on land *"... and God saw that it was good."* (Gen. 1:25). Then God continued his work on that day and made man in his own image, *"And God blessed them, and God said unto them, Be fruitful, and multiply"* (Gen. 1:28), and after giving out some rules about their vegetarian diet, and the relationship between man and animals *"God saw every thing that he had made, and, behold, it was very good."* (Gen. 1:31).

On each of these days, except the second day, God says that what he had made was good, meaning it was how he intended it to be. The second day was also good because God looked at all his creation at the end of the sixth day and saw that it was very good. So everything was as God had intended.

The question is, did God intend that his creation should include death? The answer is yes, but only in the case of plants, and possibly some of the lower forms of animals that are incapable of consciousness, although this is a hypothetical situation that we will deal with on page 14. Plants were created as food for animals and humans, without any kind of consciousness, and they do not suffer any distress when they are cut down and chewed up for food, so God's perfect creation includes the death of plants.

The status of both animals and humans is defined in terms of a blessing that is given only to them and not to the plants. Humans are given a status of dominion over the animals, but they both share a common blessing, given on the fifth and sixth days of creation, and we will look at these days in full.

> And God said, Let the waters bring forth abundantly the moving creature that hath life, and fowl that may fly above the earth in the open firmament of heaven. And God created great whales, and every living creature that moveth, which the waters brought forth abundantly, after their kind, and every winged fowl after his kind: and God saw that it was good. And God blessed them, saying, Be fruitful, and multiply, and fill the waters in the seas, and let fowl multiply in the earth. And the evening and the morning were the fifth day.
>
> And God said, Let the earth bring forth the living creature after his kind, cattle, and creeping thing, and beast of the earth after his kind: and it was so. And God made the beast of the earth after his kind, and cattle after their kind, and every thing that creepeth upon the earth after his kind: and God saw that it was good. And God said, Let us make man in our image, after our likeness: and let them have dominion over the fish of the sea, and over the fowl of the air, and over the cattle, and over all the earth, and over every creeping thing that creepeth upon the earth. So God created man in his own image, in the image of God created he him; male and female created he them. And God blessed them, and God said unto them, Be fruitful, and multiply, and replenish the earth, and subdue it: and have dominion over the fish of the sea, and over the fowl of the air, and over every living thing that moveth upon the earth. And God said, Behold, I have given you every herb bearing seed, which is upon the face of all the earth, and every tree, in the which is the fruit of a tree yielding seed; to you it shall be for meat. And to every beast of the earth, and to every fowl of the air, and to every thing that creepeth upon the earth, wherein there is life, I have given every green herb for meat: and it was so. And God saw every thing that he had made, and, behold, it was very good. And the evening and the morning were the sixth day.
>
> *Gen. 1:20-31*

If God blessed both the animals and humans, how could they be under a sentence of death? We currently live in a world where nature is red in tooth and claw, where animals tear each other apart and eat each other alive. Animals live in perpetual fear of being preyed upon, and humans also used to live in fear of wild beasts, until they learned how to live in walled cities to protect themselves. Now we live in fear of each other, and have done so throughout our entire history, as we are divided into tribes and nations that are frequently at war.

Clearly this was not the condition of animals and humans before the fall. At that time they lived together in peace, and they were vegetarian. Humans did not eat animals, and animals did not eat each other, and there is no reason to believe that they died of natural causes. There is no mention of death, and we would not expect it, because they lived under God's blessing of life, not under the curse of death that has afflicted both man and the whole of nature after the fall.

Evolutionists would argue that death is normal, and it is essential for the development of new forms of life, under the rules of natural selection and survival of the fittest. But there is none of this in the Bible. Instead we see blessings for both man and beast.

The blessings for animals and humans on the fifth and sixth days both say that they should multiply and fill the earth. However, the blessing upon man goes further, that they should subdue the earth, and have dominion over every living thing that moves. Not only is their blessing of a different order, but their status in relation to God is also different. They were created *"in the image of God"* meaning that they participated in the nature of God, with creative qualities, and they were responsible to God for all their actions.

Moving on to Genesis 2, we are given more detail about the creation of man.

> And the Lord God formed man of the dust of the ground, and breathed into his nostrils the breath of life; and man became a living soul.
>
> *Gen. 2:7*

Man is not unique in having the breath of life, or the living soul. The Hebrew *nephesh chayah*, which means "breath of life", "living

9

soul", or "living creature" is also used in Genesis 1 to describe animals, and we will discuss this further on page 12. However, there is something different about the way that life was given to man. We are told that God breathed into his nostrils the breath of life, implying a much more personal contact. The same breath of life was imparted to the woman, because she came out of the man. We have already seen that the man is described as both singular and plural, in the phrase *"... in the image of God created he him; male and female created he them."* (Gen. 1:27).

Since Adam and Eve were created in the image of God, in a way that made them responsible to God, there had to be a test to see if they would be obedient. There would be no point having a pair of robots, programmed to do whatever they were told to do. They had to be given free will, with the ability to obey or disobey, and they were given the understanding that disobedience meant death. The first mention of death in the Bible is the commandment not to eat the forbidden fruit:

> And the Lord God commanded the man, saying, Of every tree of the garden thou mayest freely eat: But of the tree of the knowledge of good and evil, thou shalt not eat of it: for in the day that thou eatest thereof thou shalt surely die.
>
> *Gen. 2:16-17*

There are a number of Hebrew words in the Bible that mean "death", but the word used here is *muth* which means plain, ordinary death and not some kind of spiritual death. We soon find out what sort of death it is when Adam and Eve take the forbidden fruit and God pronounces curses on them. The curse on Adam is as follows:

> And unto Adam he said, Because thou hast hearkened unto the voice of thy wife, and hast eaten of the tree, of which I commanded thee, saying, Thou shalt not eat of it: cursed is the ground for thy sake; in sorrow shalt thou eat of it all the days of thy life; Thorns also and thistles shall it bring forth to thee; and thou shalt eat the herb of the field; In the sweat of thy face shalt thou eat bread, till thou return unto the ground; for out of it wast thou taken: for dust thou art, and unto dust shalt thou return.
>
> *Gen. 3:17-19*

Returning to the dust means physical death, but he didn't die immediately, as soon as he took the fruit. Instead he was told that the vegetation, provided for him to eat, would not grow abundantly any more, and would have to be continually cultivated to prevent it from being stifled by thorns and thistles. He would work by the sweat of his brow, and would eventually die.

In that case we have to consider what exactly is meant by the following:

> ... in the day that thou eatest thereof thou shalt surely die.
>
> *Gen. 2:17*

What was supposed to have happened on the day that Adam took the fruit? What kind of death did he die? There can only be one possible answer to this question. He lost his immortality. The process of death and decay was implemented as soon as he took the forbidden fruit, and it continued until he finally returned to the dust, 930 years later. When someone says "I am dying", they mean they are close to the point of death, but we are all dying all the time, from the day of our conception onwards, because that's when the ageing process begins.

The loss of immortality is affirmed when Adam is thrown out of the Garden of Eden, and denied access to the tree of life.

> And the Lord God said, Behold, the man is become as one of us, to know good and evil: and now, lest he put forth his hand, and take also of the tree of life, and eat, and live for ever: Therefore the Lord God sent him forth from the garden of Eden, to till the ground from whence he was taken. So he drove out the man; and he placed at the east of the garden of Eden Cherubim,[3] and a flaming sword which turned every way, to keep the way of the tree of life.
>
> *Gen. 3:22-24*

---

[3] The KJAV says *Cherubims*, although this is a double plural. In Hebrew, *Cherub* is singular and *Cherubim* is plural. The addition of "s" gives us an Anglicised version of the Hebrew which sounds rather strange, so we stick to *Cherubim*.

11

Clearly he had access to the tree of life, before the fall, because it was in the Garden of Eden and it was evidently the source of his immortality.

> And out of the ground made the Lord God to grow every tree that is pleasant to the sight, and good for food; the tree of life also in the midst of the garden, and the tree of knowledge of good and evil.
>
> *Gen. 2:9*

Now we return to the question of animals, and how they were affected by the fall. They were blessed with life, just as man had been blessed, so they must also have been immortal, as man was immortal, but man had the special position of being made in the image of God, and therefore directly responsible to God. The animals were under the dominion of man, and were affected by his actions, so that when man came under the sentence of death, so did the animals. It might seem unfair that animals should suffer as a consequence of the sin of man, but it shows the seriousness of sin, and how the whole of creation has been affected by it. The first recorded death of an animal was when God made skins as a covering for Adam and Eve.

> Unto Adam also and to his wife did the Lord God make coats of skins, and clothed them.
>
> *Gen. 3:21*

Nephesh Life

Animal and human life is defined in Genesis 1 and 2 by *nephesh* which means "breath" or "soul" and *chayah* which means "living thing". We have already seen some of the verses where these words appear, but here they are again with the Hebrew inserted:

> And God said, Let the waters bring forth abundantly the moving creature that hath life [*nephesh chayah*], and fowl that may fly above the earth in the open firmament of heaven. And God created great whales, and every living creature [*nephesh chayah*] that moveth, which the waters brought forth abundantly, after their kind, and every winged fowl after his kind: and God saw that it was good.
>
> *Gen. 1:20-21*

12

And God said, Let the earth bring forth the living creature [*nephesh chayah*] after his kind, cattle, and creeping thing, and beast of the earth after his kind: and it was so.

Gen. 1:24

So God created man in his own image ... and God said unto them ... have dominion over the fish of the sea, and over the fowl of the air, and over every living thing [*chayah*] that moveth upon the earth.

Gen. 1:27-28

And to every beast[4] [*chayah*] of the earth, and to every fowl of the air, and to every thing that creepeth upon the earth, wherein there is life [*nephesh chayah*], I have given every green herb for meat: and it was so.

Gen. 1:30

And the Lord God formed man of the dust of the ground, and breathed into his nostrils the breath of life [*nishmat chayim*];[5] and man became a living soul [*nephesh chayah*].

Gen. 2:7

The word *nephesh* normally refers to humans and air-breathing animals, but from the events of the fifth day of creation, we see that it also includes fish, and this is even more apparent if we look at the literal English of the American Standard Version.

And God said, Let the waters swarm with swarms of living creatures [*nephesh chayah*], and let birds fly above the earth in the open firmament of heaven. And God created the great sea-monsters, and every living creature [*nephesh chayah*] that moveth, wherewith the waters swarmed, after their kind, and every winged bird after its kind: and God saw that it was good.

Gen. 1:20-21, ASV, 1901

Nephesh life is also characterised by the possession of blood, and when Noah came out of the ark, after the flood, he was told that this is the substance that defines life.

---

[4] Literally "living thing" but translated "beast" because it is of the earth.
[5] A variation of the grammar, but the meaning is essentially unchanged.

> Every moving thing that liveth [*chai*][6] shall be meat for you; even as the green herb have I given you all things. But flesh with the life [*nephesh*] thereof, which is the blood thereof, shall ye not eat.
>
> *Gen. 9:3-4*

This is the first time that specific permission was given to eat animals, and it probably reflects the much harsher conditions of the post-flood world, where the correct type of vegetables do not always grow in sufficient quantity. Vegetarians today depend on a wide variety of imports from various parts of the world and would probably revert to eating meat if they had to live entirely from local produce.

We are specifically commanded not to eat the blood, because this is the vital component that gives life. The blood supply carries oxygen and nutrients to all parts of the body, including the brain which is the seat of consciousness. Even the heart is of only secondary importance, and can be stopped for medical surgery as long as the blood is kept circulating by artificial means.

Lower Life Forms

The word *nephesh* is used elsewhere in the Old Testament, sometimes to describe animal and human life, the same as in the creation story, but very often to describe pleasure, pain and various emotional conditions that imply consciousness, for example:

> My soul [*nephesh*] is also sore vexed: but thou, O Lord, how long?
>
> *Psalm 6:3*

> And my soul [*nephesh*] shall be joyful in the Lord: it shall rejoice in his salvation.
>
> *Psalm 35:9*

The association of *nephesh* with consciousness might suggest that certain types of primitive animals do not have *nephesh* life in the true sense of the word, and their deaths are inconsequential. In that case, some of them could have died before the fall, and the creation

---

[6] The root word from which chayah and chayim are derived.

would still be considered "good", because there was no pain or suffering. For example, a monkey could tread on an insect and kill it, but the death of the insect would be inconsequential because it has no consciousness. The question is, how do we define which animals are conscious and which ones are not? We can reasonably believe that dogs and cats are conscious because they respond to human activity in sophisticated ways that go beyond mere instinctive reactions, and they appear to feel pleasure and pain. It's not so easy to identify consciousness in the case of insects, worms, and fish.

We also have to consider what sort of "blessing" could be given to primitive animals, on the fifth and sixth days of creation, if they did not possess consciousness. What's the point of being blessed if you don't know about it? Either the animals were all conscious, and some mechanism was in place, before the fall, to protect insects and other vulnerable animals, or else there were unconscious animals that could die without suffering, and the blessing applies only to higher animals that have consciousness.

All of these arguments are, of course, dependent on the supposition that the pre-fall world was much the same as the world in which we live, but clearly it was not. If we have to ask whether or not a monkey could tread on an insect and kill it, we also have to consider whether or not a tree could fall on Adam. He was immortal, in the sense that he was not subject to ageing and decay, but could he get killed in an accident? Clearly he could not, because he used to walk with God in the garden, and in the purely hypothetical event that a tree was capable of falling, God would have either restrained it by his power, or else would have made Adam indestructible so that he could not be hurt by a falling tree. If God could protect Adam, he could also protect an insect that is in danger of being trampled on by a monkey. We know, in any case, that even in this present world that is full of death and destruction, a sparrow does not fall unless God sees it. (Matt. 10:29).

The most likely explanation, that makes the most sense, is that Adam had a body that was similar to the resurrection body of Jesus, capable of changing from one form to another, and we will deal with this question on page 37. If Adam got crushed by a tree, he could disappear and re-appear somewhere else, totally healed. He would feel no pain because he would have no need for it. Pain is a messaging system that tells us there is a problem with our bodies that needs attention. The sharper the pain, the more urgent is the need for a remedy, and it causes us to rest and avoid placing stress on the affected area. Adam had no need for pain, and in the purely hypothetical situation that he got injured, he would be instantly healed.

We are not told very much about what the animals were like before the fall. It appears that the word *nephesh* applies to all of them, so perhaps they all had consciousness, but we cannot know for sure. If they did, they would be protected from injury, just as Adam was protected. Whatever happened, we can be sure of one thing, that they were all affected by the fall. Even the plants were affected by the fall, because thorns and thistles began to grow, making it difficult to cultivate crops. Did Adam ever get stung by a bee before the fall? Did he get bitten by a mosquito? If he did, he would not have suffered pain for reasons already explained, but there would be no reason for such an event. The aggressive capabilities of animals, from the most primitive to the most intelligent, all came as a consequence of the fall. When the effects of the fall are cancelled, we will return to the conditions of Eden, and even before we reach that stage, during a period of partial restoration called the millennium, a child will be able to play in a snake pit. (see page 63).

Physical and Spiritual Death

Now that we have looked at the effects of the fall on the whole of creation, including humans, animals and plants, we move on to the question of physical and spiritual death. Some Evangelicals attempt to define spiritual death as if it was totally separate from physical death, but the Bible teaches no such thing, either in the Old Testament or the New Testament. Instead there is physical death, but it has a spiritual context.

The first mention of death is the commandment not to eat the forbidden fruit, as we have already seen:

> ... in the day that thou eatest thereof thou shalt surely die.
>
> *Gen. 2:17*

16

There are a number of Hebrew words that mean "death", and this passage uses the most common one, which is *muth*. There are many occurrences of this word in the Bible, and it always means physical death, although there is sometimes a spiritual context. In this case we know it means physical death because, as we have already seen, Adam is told he will "return to the dust" because of his sin.

If some kind of spiritual separation from God was intended, the word *muth* would not have been used. Instead we would have a passage similar to the banishment of Cain:

> When thou tillest the ground, it shall not henceforth yield unto thee her strength; a fugitive and a vagabond shalt thou be in the earth. And Cain said unto the Lord, My punishment is greater than I can bear. Behold, thou hast driven me out this day from the face of the earth; and from thy face shall I be hid; and I shall be a fugitive and a vagabond in the earth; ... And Cain went out from the presence of the Lord, and dwelt in the land of Nod, on the east of Eden.
>
> *Gen. 4:12-16*

Sometimes *muth* can mean the fear of death, or circumstances closely associated with it, for example:

- At the time of Moses, when the firstborn of the Egyptians were all dead, the Egyptians prevailed upon the Israelites to leave quickly, saying *"We be all dead men"*. (Exodus 12:33).

- There was a wealthy man called Nabal who despised the men of David when they came to visit him. David was offended and ready to go to war, but Nabal's wife Abigail came with offerings of peace. Nabal knew nothing about the threat of war, but when Abigail told him, *"... his heart died within him, and he became as a stone. And it came to pass about ten days after, that the Lord smote Nabal, that he died."* (1 Sam. 25:37-38). Clearly Nabal must have had a heart attack or a stroke, and it left him paralysed, and it was considered to be a type of death, but then he died ten days later.

The nearest we get to spiritual death is in the following passage from Ezekiel, who was taken captive into Babylon, although this might also mean physical death because of the violence of the captivity.

> Behold, all souls are mine; as the soul of the father, so also the soul of the son is mine: the soul that sinneth, it shall die. But if a man be just, and do that which is lawful and right, ... he shall surely live, saith the Lord God.
>
> *Ezek. 18:4-9*

Whether this passage can be partially or wholly spiritualised, the "soul" must be the *nephesh* life that we have already discussed, rather than some spiritual quality. The context of the passage suggests that the issue of greatest concern is the spiritual state of the person at the point of death, rather than the timing and circumstances of the death itself.

Daniel, who was also a captive in Babylon, wrote about the status of the dead as follows:

> And many of them that sleep in the dust of the earth shall awake, some to everlasting life, and some to shame and everlasting contempt.
>
> *Dan. 12:2*

This, at last, gives us a clear statement about spiritual life, in the context of the resurrection of the dead, which is a repeated theme in the New Testament. We can compare it with the following New Testament passage:

> Martha saith unto him, I know that he shall rise again in the resurrection at the last day. Jesus said unto her, I am the resurrection, and the life: he that believeth in me, though he were dead, yet shall he live: And whosoever liveth and believeth in me shall never die. Believest thou this?
>
> *John 11:24-26*

How is it possible to say that someone will "never die"? Obviously it means that the person will never die without remedy, and the same applies to any spiritual interpretations of the passage in Ezekiel. The soul that sins will die without remedy, and the righteous will live, meaning they will rise to everlasting life.

A number of other words are used in the Old Testament, to represent death.

- *Nephesh* normally means the breath of life, but sometimes it means a dead body, or more precisely, a body from which the breath of life has departed. It is sometimes used in the laws prohibiting contact with a dead body, for example *"There shall none be defiled for the dead among his people"*. (Lev. 21:1).

- *Rephaim* is the name of a people, supposed to be giants, who lived to the east of the Dead Sea, but it was also used to mean the assembly of the departed spirits. It is sometimes used metaphorically, for example *"The man that wandereth out of the way of understanding shall remain in the congregation of the dead."* (Prov. 21:16).

The New Testament contains a number of words that mean "death", but the most common one is *thanatos* which appears as follows:

> For the wages of sin is death; but the gift of God is eternal life through Jesus Christ our Lord.
>
> *Rom. 6:23*

Normally, *thanatos* simply means "death", but in this case it means death with a spiritual context. It refers to the sentence of death that we are all under, as a consequence of Adam's sin, but it is not death without remedy. Physical death is being compared with the resurrection to eternal life.

Thanatos is sometimes used in a metaphorical sense, for example being "dead to the law". The following verse uses the word *thanatoo* which means to "become dead" and contrasts it with a phrase that uses, *nekros*, another word that means "death".

> Wherefore, my brethren, ye also are become dead [*thanatoo*] to the law by the body of Christ; that ye should be married to another, even to him who is raised from the dead [*nekros*], that we should bring forth fruit unto God.
>
> *Rom. 7:4*

Nekros is used quite commonly, and it normally means physical death, but it is sometimes used metaphorically, and the two types of death occur alongside each other in the phrase *"let the dead [nekros] bury their dead [nekros]."* (Matt. 8:22). The metaphorical use of *nekros* can be compared with the verse we have seen already, where someone without understanding is considered to be *"in the congregation of the dead".* (Prov. 21:16).

Apothnesko is another commonly used word, and it means "to die away", referring to the process of death, but often it just means "dead". It is sometimes used to mean recent death, for example when Jairus's daughter was raised (Mark 5:35-39). Also, when Jesus died, the centurion asked a question about how long he had been dead. (Mark 15:44). It is sometimes used metaphorically, for example *"... if ye be dead with Christ from the rudiments of the world, ..."* (Col. 2:20).

So we see that in the Bible there are all sorts of death phrases that mean physical death, or some kind of spiritual or metaphorical meaning is implied. The rule to be followed is that a word must always be given its literal meaning, unless some other meaning is clearly implied, and for all the words considered so far, we have the result that the vast majority of death phrases mean literal, physical death. If you want to go into this further, you need a Bible concordance such as Young's or Strong's, which separates out the different Hebrew and Greek words and gives their meaning. You will find that there are phrases that imply spiritual death, but really it's the spiritual context of physical death, and we always have to take into account that the reason we die, physically, is because of sin. Our spiritual condition determines what happens when the dead are raised, either to eternal life or eternal contempt.

Physical and Spiritual Life

We have already looked at *nephesh* life in some detail, and we have seen that it applies to all human and animal life, at least in the creation narrative. It also refers to states of mind that imply consciousness, for example David, the writer of the Psalms, said that his soul could be "vexed" or "joyful". This is an expression of the quality of life, not the mere existence of it, and such expressions are commonplace in the Bible.

The concept of life is almost exclusively defined in Hebrew by the word *chai*, which becomes *chayah* or *chayim*, depending on the grammar, and as we have seen, it is sometimes combined with *nephesh* to mean "breath of life". It is difficult to find a single occasion where it can be unambiguously spiritualised, not even in the following verse:

> ... man doth not live [*chayah*] by bread only, but by every word that proceedeth out of the mouth of the Lord doth man live [*chayah*].
>
> *Deut. 8:3*

Comparing this with another passage in the same book, where we are encouraged to "choose life", we might think we have good material for a sermon about spiritual life, until we find out the circumstances in which we have to choose between life and death.

> I call heaven and earth to record this day against you, that I have set before you life [*chayim*] and death [*muth*], blessing and cursing: therefore choose life [*chayim*], that both thou and thy seed may live [*chayah*]:
>
> *Deut. 30:19*

This comes after a long list of blessings and curses, beginning in Deuteronomy 28. There are blessings of safety, security and material prosperity for obedience to the law, and curses of extreme poverty and deprivation for disobedience. The curses are so severe that it is doubtful that anyone could physically survive them. The instruction to live by the word of God, and not by bread alone, means quite literally that we need to live according to God's word to stay physically alive.

Turning to the New Testament, we see a different perspective on things, because there is a more distinct difference between physical and spiritual life.

The Greek word *psuche*[7] means human and animal life, breath or soul. It seems to be much the same as the Hebrew *nephesh chayah*, but here is an example that uses it in more than one way:

> For whosoever will save his life [*psuche*] shall lose it: and whosoever will lose his life [*psuche*] for my sake shall find it. For what is a man profited, if he shall gain the whole world, and lose his own soul [*psuche*]? Or what shall a man give in exchange for his soul [*psuche*]?
>
> *Matt. 16:25-26*

Some literal translations use the word "life", or "soul" consistently throughout the whole passage, so that it is not obvious what is being gained and what is being lost. The King James Authorised Version and most other non-literal translations are more helpful, using "life" for the first two occurrences of *psuche* and "soul" for the second two. The "soul" means the personality or consciousness, and the notion of gaining the world and losing your soul can be applied to all sorts of different situations. For example, a salesman might be expected to say things on behalf of his company that he knows are not true. For a while he might go through the routine because he needs the money, but eventually he gets tired of telling lies, so he quits and finds another job that offers a greater sense of personal satisfaction. Obviously Jesus offers a lot more than just personal satisfaction, but the "soul", in the most general sense, is the consciousness that enables us to experience a variety of emotions.

Another commonly used Greek word is *zoe* which means life, motion or activity. It is sometimes used to describe the manner in which we live, for example:

> And not many days after the younger son gathered all together, and took his journey into a far country, and there wasted his substance with riotous living [*zoe*].
>
> *Luke 15:13*

---

[7] Together with *logos*, meaning 'word', this gives us 'psychology'.

Therefore we are buried with him by baptism into death: that like as Christ was raised up from the dead by the glory of the Father, even so we also should walk in newness of life [*zoe*].

Rom. 6:4

And when the tempter came to him, he said, If thou be the Son of God, command that these stones be made bread. But he answered and said, It is written, Man shall not live [*zoe*] by bread alone, but by every word that proceedeth out of the mouth of God.

Matt. 4:3-4

In this last verse, Jesus is quoting from Deut. 8:3 that we have already seen, and the Hebrew *chayah* is replaced by the Greek *zoe*, indicating the manner of life and not just its existence. Of course Jesus didn't actually speak these words in Greek. He spoke Aramaic and the Gospels were subsequently written in Greek (although Matthew's Gospel, and possibly some of the other Gospels, are thought to have first been written in Hebrew[8]).

Jesus and the Apostles frequently used the word *zoe* to mean life that extends into the future, or is to be gained in the future, for example "eternal life", or the "crown of life".

My sheep hear my voice, and I know them, and they follow me: And I give unto them eternal life [*zoe*]; and they shall never perish, neither shall any man pluck them out of my hand.

John 10:27-28

Blessed is the man that endureth temptation: for when he is tried, he shall receive the crown of life [*zoe*], which the Lord hath promised to them that love him.

James 1:12

Expressions like this are so frequent in the New Testament that, as far as the early Christians were concerned, they represented the normal use of the word *zoe* and not the exception. Now, at last, we have found something unambiguously spiritual, and we find that it is not for this life alone, but for eternity.

---

[8] Bivin, D., Blizzard, R.B., *Understanding the Difficult Words of Jesus.*

The reason for going through all these words has been to find out what the Bible means when it talks about life and death, so that we can gain a better understanding of what sort of death Adam suffered during the fall, and what sort of life might be offered as a remedy. We have found that in both Hebrew and Greek, when the Bible talks about life and death, it normally refers to our physical existence in this world, and spiritualises it only in exceptional cases. Then when we get to the Greek word *zoe*, we find the opposite. The early Christians were so much focused on eternal life (*zoe aionios*), and spoke about it so frequently, that it became the normal use of the word *zoe*. We will soon go into the details of what they believed, and we will find that it was something more that just the departure of the soul to a spiritual realm at the point of death. They believed in the resurrection of the dead, with immortal bodies, and the eventual creation of a New Heaven and a New Earth where the believers would dwell for ever. This is offered as a complete remedy for the fall, and therefore we have the inescapable conclusion that the fall involved the loss of physical immortality.

Adam's Lost Reward

There are some Christians who believe that humanity was created mortal, but would be given immortality, depending on the result of a test. Adam and Eve were told not to eat of the forbidden fruit, and if they were obedient, they would be rewarded with immortality. They failed the test and never claimed their reward, but the plan of salvation was put in place so that immortality would be available through grace and not through merit.

While this sounds very reasonable, and conveniently accommodates evolution with the hope of immortality, it is not what the Bible teaches. We have already seen that death is not part of the created order, except for plants that were created for food, but there are other problems with this doctrine.

Adam is never presented as merely an under-achiever, who failed to gain a reward. He is presented as someone who brought death.

> Wherefore, as by one man sin entered into the world, and death by sin;
> and so death passed upon all men, for that all have sinned:
>
> *Rom. 5:12*

This verse specifically says that death came into the world through sin, which means it was not in the world already. The entry of death into the world is very different from failing to get rid of it.

Death is never presented as part of the perfect will of God, not even temporarily as part of the creation scenario. It exists as a consequence of sin, and operates more or less indiscriminately in a fallen world. It is seen as the work of the devil, and it will be cast into the lake of fire, together with the devil, at the Final Judgement.

> And the devil that deceived them was cast into the lake of fire and
> brimstone, ... And death and hell were cast into the lake of fire. This is
> the second death.
>
> *Rev. 20:10-14*

The word for "hell" is *hades*, which is the Greek equivalent of the Hebrew *sheol*. It is the place where the dead wait for the resurrection. It will serve no purpose after the Final Judgement, and will be cast into the lake of fire, together with death.

The "second death" is a the ultimate fate of Satan and those who serve him, but death as we know it will be abolished. It is part of the domain of Satan, and he was given authority to use it after Adam sinned, but after the Final Judgement he will take it with him to the lake of fire.

> The last enemy that shall be destroyed is death.
>
> *1 Cor. 15:26*

Recovery from the Fall

Now that we have gone through the Biblical issues of life and death, and we have seen how we were reduced to mortality as a consequence of Adam's sin, we have to consider what this means for the purpose of preaching and evangelism.

Obviously at the Billy Graham meetings we didn't go through the early chapters of Genesis in so much detail, and we didn't go through the rest of the Bible giving Hebrew and Greek definitions of death, because it would all have been much too complicated. Normally it wasn't necessary to look at Genesis at all, because people understood well enough what was meant by "death" and "eternal life". They knew that we were offering them something that extends beyond the grave, and they would live in the presence of God forever. In many cases they knew a lot more than that, but we focused on what was needed to get them saved, and for the time being that was enough.

Later on, as they went to church and spent time studying their Bibles, they would learn more about what eternal life means, and how we wait for the return of Jesus, and the resurrection of the dead, and finally the New Heaven and New Earth, with the New Jerusalem where there is the tree of life that annihilates the curse of sin altogether. Everything will return to its former state of perfection, as it was in the Garden of Eden before the Fall.

The Jewish Wedding Customs

It may seem like a strange diversion, to go through the Jewish wedding customs at this point, but Jesus and the Apostles frequently referred to them when describing the plan of salvation. If we understand these customs, we can map out the complete sequence of events, from the earliest prophetic announcement of the Messiah, to his death and resurrection, then his return and the establishment of his kingdom.

The Jewish wedding customs, in Biblical times, involved a contract that was arranged between the families of the bride and groom, primarily between the respective fathers who considered themselves to be responsible for finding marriage partners for their sons and daughters. The father of the groom would normally initiate the process in one of three ways.

- He could personally go and see the bride's father, normally accompanied by his son, and would present a contract.
- He could send a trusted agent to make the arrangements, for example Abraham sent his servant to find a wife for his son Isaac. (Gen. 24).

- The groom could go and present the contract himself, but only with the authority of his father. For example, Isaac sent his son Jacob to Padan-aram, to find a wife from among the daughters of Laban, his brother-in-law. It didn't turn out entirely as expected, because Jacob ended up marrying two of Laban's daughters, a consequence that would have been much less likely if Isaac had personally been there and chosen the prospective bride. (Gen. 28:2; 29:1-30). When Jesus came into this world he personally presented his marriage contract to his bride, on the authority of his Father, although it was not prone to error as in Jacob's contract, because his Father's instructions were much more explicit and he was fully obedient. *"... the Son can do nothing of himself, but what he sees the Father doing. For whatever things he does, these the Son also does likewise."* (John 5:19, World English Bible[9]).

Assuming that the groom is fully involved in the process from the beginning, the wedding customs, described by Zola Levitt[10], are as follows:

The groom would first go to the bride's family and offer a contract for her, which included a price to be paid. The reason for the bride price is because, in an agricultural society, girls were not raised to work on the farm or family business. Instead they were raised to be good wives and keep the house, and the girl's father had to be compensated for the effort he had made in raising her.

If the girl's father agreed with the contract, he would ask the girl, and if she agreed, the groom would pour out a cup of wine for her. She would indicate her acceptance by taking the cup, and the groom would also have some wine. Then he would pay the price, and from that point on, they were "betrothed". Then he would leave, but first he would make a speech, saying something like "I go to prepare a place for you". He would return to his father's house and decorate a room, or perhaps build a small annexe to the house. He would make

---

[9] *World English Bible*, <http://ebible.org>.
[10] Levitt, Zola, *A Christian Love Story*.

it look really good, because this would be his wedding chamber where he would spend his first few days of marriage with his new bride. While he is working on his chamber, the girl would prepare for herself a wedding dress and she would keep it somewhere, ready for use at short notice, because she did not know when she would need it. She might even sleep in her wedding dress, in anticipation of the groom's return. She would also keep a lamp with some oil in it, ready for a journey at night, and her female friends would also have their lamps ready, so that they could accompany her.

The groom would continue building and decorating his wedding chamber, and his father would occasionally inspect it to see if it was ready. The groom would not be able to go and get his bride until the chamber was finished to the father's satisfaction. If anyone asked the groom when was the day of the wedding, he would say "Only my father knows".

When the father decided that everything was ready, the groom would set off during the night to the bride's house, together with his friends, but they wouldn't barge straight in. When they got near the house, someone would shout with a loud voice "The bridegroom is coming". This was the signal that the bride should get herself ready and make herself look good, and her friends would help her, but they didn't have much time. Soon the groom would enter the house and take her away, and his friends would accompany the girls who were with her. This event is called the *abduction of the bride*. The party would proceed to the groom's house, carrying their lamps because it was dark and they had to find their way.

It was from this wedding procession that Jesus derived his parable of the wise and foolish virgins. (Matt. 25:1-13). The wise virgins kept oil in their lamps, but the foolish ones didn't. They went out to buy oil at the last minute but got back too late and missed the procession, and were locked out of the wedding.

When the procession got to the groom's house, the groom would take his bride into his wedding chamber, and would shut the door, and they would consummate the marriage. One special guest called the "friend of the bridegroom", (the oriental equivalent of the "best man"), would wait outside the door, for a signal from the groom, to say the marriage is consummated, then he would announce it to the other guests and they would all start to celebrate. They would continue to celebrate for seven days, and on the seventh day the bride and groom would come out and join them, for the event known as the "marriage supper", where a much larger number of guests would be present.

When the festivities were ended and the guests had gone home, the bride and groom would go to their own house where they would live permanently.

In these marriage customs, we see how Christ becomes married to his church:

- The contract for our redemption was offered under the authority of the Father, who had already made known his will through many Messianic prophecies.

- Jesus came and sealed the contract by offering the cup of redemption to his disciples at the Passover festival,[11] then he paid the price of our sins on the cross.

- He rose from the dead and met with his disciples on a few occasions, then he ascended and returned to his Father in heaven.

- Now he is preparing a place for us in his Father's house. (John 14:2-3). At the same time we are waiting for him to take us away, and we have to keep ourselves ready.

- When he comes, we will all rise and meet him, both the living and the dead, an event known as the *"rapture"*.

- We will become his consummated bride, and will emerge from his wedding chamber to celebrate the Marriage Supper, together with many other guests.

- He will take us to his dwelling place, first to rule and reign with him on Earth in the Millennial Kingdom (a period of a thousand years when Satan is bound), then, after the creation of a New Heaven and a New Earth, we will live with him for ever in the perfect world.

---

[11] This was one day before the actual Passover, when he would not be there.

In this scenario, the "bride" consists of only the believers who have lived during the church age, that is, from the day of Pentecost when the church began, until the Rapture. The Old Testament believers will be guests at the Marriage Supper, and there might also be another group called the tribulation saints who we will discuss later. John the Baptist was the last of the Old Testament believers and he did not consider himself to be part of the bride. Instead he called himself the *"friend of the bridegroom"* who rejoices when he hears the bridegroom's voice (John 3:29). Clearly, he is the special guest who announces the consummation of the marriage.

Arnold Fruchtenbaum[12] gives us a very similar account of the Jewish wedding customs, but with some small differences. When the bride and groom arrive at the groom's house, they have a Wedding Ceremony, to which only a few people are invited, followed by the Marriage Supper which lasts for seven days. There are probably other variations, as the customs are not always the same from one place to another.

Now that we have looked at the wedding customs, we can return to our main purpose, which is to map out the sequence of events that lead to our complete redemption.

The Protevangelic Prophecy

The plan of salvation, which leads eventually to the complete cancellation of all the effects of the fall, was put in place at the time of the fall itself. The Lord pronounced a curse on the serpent as follows:

> And I will put enmity between thee and the woman, and between thy seed and her seed; it shall bruise thy head, and thou shalt bruise his heel.
>
> *Gen. 3:15*

This prophecy, known as the *'Protevangel'* is a description of the Messiah, who would fight against the serpent, and would be injured

---

[12] Fruchtenbaum, A., *The Jewish Wedding System and the Bride of Christ.*

in the process, but would make a comeback and inflict a much greater injury on the serpent, annihilating his power altogether. The Messiah would be bruised only in the heel, but the serpent would be bruised in the head.

When Jesus died on the cross, he was indeed injured in the heel, because this is how the Romans used to drive in the nails. The feet would be placed sideways on the cross and the nails were driven through the ankle, between the leg-bone and the foot. He was also injured in the wrists as the nails were driven between the two bones of the forearm. After a few hours of this excruciating torment, he died on the cross, but he rose from the dead, able to offer life to those who believed in him. This was the signal that the serpent's days were numbered. The serpent still wreaks havoc all over the world, persecuting the believers, but Jesus will return and crush his head.

The Messiah is described as the seed of the woman, but not the seed of the man. All the sons of Adam are under the curse of sin, and we know how it works in practice, because any parent can tell you, we learn how to sin before we can even crawl. The Messiah was not the seed of man, and therefore not under the curse, but he was fully human because he was the seed of the woman, and therefore able to give us salvation.

The reason for choosing the woman as the natural parent of the Messiah, and excluding the man, has got nothing to do with the well-worn arguments about who was most responsible for the fall. It is God's response to the serpent, who aimed his deception directly at the woman, hoping that he could take over the world entirely and use her as an ally against God. It was therefore appropriate that God should show who was in control, and he used the woman to bring the Messiah into the world. The sin nature is passed on when children are born to men and women in the natural way, but when God chose only a woman to give birth, he brought into the world a special child with his own nature.

Since the Protevangelic prophecy was given, it was passed on to the descendants of Adam and Eve so that other cultures around the world anticipated the arrival of a hero-figure who would fight against the serpent and would eventually crush its head, but would get injured in the process. This has appeared, in various distortions of the tale, in pagan mythology. Probably the most famous example is Hercules who fought against the Hydra, the serpent from the swamp of Lerna which had nine heads, one of them immortal. He smashed its mortal heads with his club, but in place of each head, two grew up. Iolaus, his charioteer, came to his aid with a firebrand, burning the roots of the heads to prevent them from growing. Then Hercules cut off the immortal head and buried it, placing a heavy rock on it. During the battle, the Hydra coiled itself around his foot, and a large crab came and wounded it, but Hercules killed the crab.[13] These creatures are represented in the sky, with the large but faint constellation Hydra stretching like a snake along the northern side of four signs of the Zodiac, namely Cancer, Leo, Virgo and Libra. Cancer is the crab who comes to the aid of the Hydra.

Hercules is the son of Zeus (Jupiter) and Alcmena, so he does not appear in Greek mythology as the offspring of a virgin birth. However, we should notice that among the four constellations traversed by Hydra, we have Virgo, the virgin, carrying a sheaf of corn representing the promised seed.

There are other stories that contain variations of this drama. For example there is the constellation Orion who sets in the western sky, having been bitten by Scorpio who rises in the eastern sky. But he is brought back again by Ophiuchus, the healer and snake handler, who follows Scorpio across the sky. Scorpio disappears over the western horizon, under the foot of Ophiuchus, while Orion rises again in the east.

There is also the story of Achilles. His mother bathed him in the waters of the Styx, the river in the Underworld which makes people invulnerable. However, she held on to his heels while bathing him, leaving them untouched by the water. Then when he was grown up, he went into battle against the Trojans, with great success, until an arrow struck him in the heel and he died.

---

[13] Frazer, J. G. (editor), *Library and Epitome*, Apollodorus 2.5.2, <www.perseus.tufts.edu/cgi-bin/ptext?lookup=Apollod.+2.5.2>.

The Greeks even have a story of the fall, with the suggestion of some sort of remedy. Pandora opened her box and released all sorts of evil upon the world, but there was one thing that remained in the box, called "hope".

Jesus is, of course, the real hero that the world has been waiting for, the fulfilment of the Protevangelic prophecy, and the hope of the nations. God made his covenant with Abraham, that all the nations would be blessed through his descendants. The covenant was affirmed with his son Isaac and his grandson Jacob, the patriarch of the nation of Israel. There were various other prophecies, that the Messiah would come from the tribe of Judah, from the line of David, and they are described in detail in many study Bibles and commentaries, but here are just a few of them:

> The sceptre[14] shall not depart from Judah, nor a lawgiver from between his feet, until Shiloh come; and unto him shall the gathering of the people be.
>
> *Gen. 49:10*

> Therefore the Lord himself shall give you a sign; Behold, a virgin shall conceive, and bear a son, and shall call his name Immanuel.
>
> *Isaiah 7:14*

> Who hath believed our report? and to whom is the arm of the Lord revealed? For he hath no form nor comeliness; and when we shall see him, there is no beauty that we should desire him. He is despised and rejected of men; a man of sorrows, and acquainted with grief: and we hid as it were our faces from him; he was despised, and we esteemed him not. Surely he hath borne our griefs, and carried our sorrows: yet we did esteem him stricken, smitten of God, and afflicted. But he was wounded for our transgressions, he was bruised for our iniquities: the chastisement of our peace was upon him; and with his stripes we are healed. All we like sheep have gone astray; we have turned every one to his own way; and the Lord hath laid on him the iniquity of us all.
>
> *Isaiah 53:1-6*

---

[14] The sceptre means the authority of independent government, which the Jews lost in AD 6 when Judea was annexed to the Roman province of Syria. Shiloh is a title of the Messiah.

33

The Sacrificial System

When Adam and Eve fell, they immediately knew that they were naked and covered themselves with fig leaves. God spoke to them and pronounced the curses on them, but also gave them the hope of the Messiah. Then the Lord gave them coats, made of animal skins, because the leaves did not provide an adequate covering. These were the first animal sacrifices, made by God himself, while they were still in the Garden of Eden. Then the Lord threw them out of the garden, and placed the Cherubim with a flaming sword at the east of the garden, to prevent them from accessing the tree of life.

Then we see the first sacrifices performed by humans. Cain and his brother Abel knew that sacrifices were needed, to come near to God, and it should have been obvious, from what had happened already, that it had to be a blood sacrifice. Abel was a shepherd, so he offered a sheep from his flock, but Cain was an arable farmer, cultivating fruit. He offered some of his fruit, but the Lord would not accept it. An offering of fruit was as useless as the fig leaves that Adam and Eve had used to cover themselves. Cain became angry and killed his brother Abel, and the Lord responded to this by sending him away to the land of Nod, east of Eden. Also, the fertility of the ground would be even worse, and he would become nomadic, wandering from one place to another.

The land of Nod does not exist anywhere on the earth today, and neither does Eden, because the entire geography of the world was changed during the Flood. We know that the land of Nod was somewhere to the east of Eden in the pre-Flood world, and Cain wasn't too happy about going there, not just because of the harsh conditions, but because he would be further away from God.

> And Cain said unto the Lord, My punishment is greater than I can bear. Behold, thou hast driven me out this day from the face of the earth; and from thy face shall I be hid; ...
>
> *Gen. 4:13-14*

This gives us a hint about where they might have offered the sacrifices. Adam and Eve had been thrown out of the Garden of Eden, but God was still there. The nearest that anyone could get to

God was in front of the Cherubim, at the entrance to the Garden, where they guarded the way to the tree of life. It seems, therefore, that this was the place for offering sacrifices. Cain was obviously concerned that when he was sent away to the land of Nod, he would not be able to offer sacrifices any more.

After the Flood, the whole world was changed and there was no longer a unique place of sacrifice, but when the Israelites came out of Egypt, the Lord met with Moses on Mount Sinai and commanded him to build the mercy seat and two cherubim, made of gold, and place them above the ark of the covenant.

> And thou shalt make a mercy seat of pure gold: two cubits and a half shall be the length thereof, and a cubit and a half the breadth thereof. And thou shalt make two cherubim[15] of gold, of beaten work shalt thou make them, in the two ends of the mercy seat. And make one cherub on the one end, and the other cherub on the other end: even of the mercy seat shall ye make the cherubim on the two ends thereof. And the cherubim shall stretch forth their wings on high, covering the mercy seat with their wings, and their faces shall look one to another; toward the mercy seat shall the faces of the cherubim be. And thou shalt put the mercy seat above upon the ark; and in the ark thou shalt put the testimony that I shall give thee. And there I will meet with thee, and I will commune with thee from above the mercy seat, from between the two cherubim which are upon the ark of the testimony, of all things which I will give thee in commandment unto the children of Israel.
>
> *Exodus 25:17-22*

Clearly, the two golden cherubim were representations of the original guardians of the tree of life at the Garden of Eden. God would meet with Moses, and with his appointed priests, from between the cherubim when they went to the tabernacle to offer sacrifices.

The cherubim were a continual reminder of their place of origin, the Garden of Eden, and fostered the hope that one day, when the promised Messiah comes, they will find their way back there.

---

[15] See note 3, page 11.

There was always a special place for the Israelites to offer sacrifices. In the wilderness they had the tabernacle, and when they went over to the Promised Land, the Lord established a place for his name.

> But when ye go over Jordan, and dwell in the land which the Lord your God giveth you to inherit, and when he giveth you rest from all your enemies round about, so that ye dwell in safety; Then there shall be a place which the Lord your God shall choose to cause his name to dwell there; thither shall ye bring all that I command you; your burnt offerings, and your sacrifices, your tithes, and the heave offering of your hand, and all your choice vows which ye vow unto the Lord:
>
> *Deut. 12:10-11*

The place, of course, was Jerusalem, and the sacrificial system continued, with a few interruptions, until the time of Messiah, who was the perfect sacrifice for sin. About forty years after his crucifixion, Jerusalem was invaded by the Romans and the Temple was destroyed.

The Messiah

Jesus was fully human, born of a woman, but not born of a man, and therefore not under the curse of sin as we are (and the reasons for this have been given earlier, under the Protevangelic prophecy). Jesus offered himself as the perfect sacrifice, paying the price of our sin, through his death on the cross. He was buried and placed in a tomb, then he rose again to show that he had overcome death. This is the surest affirmation that death was not part of God's original creation, where everything was good. If death was good, why should Jesus want to overcome it?

After his resurrection he appeared to his disciples on a number of occasions, and according to the Apostle Paul he appeared to more than five hundred people at once (1 Cor. 15:6). The resurrection of Jesus is one of the most well established facts of history. It was preached relentlessly around the Roman Empire during the first century, under conditions of persecution and martyrdom. The Romans wanted to stamp out Christianity because they considered it to be a scourge upon the Empire, and they could have easily achieved their objective, by proving that Jesus had not risen from the dead, but they could not.

After Jesus had risen and appeared to his disciples, he ascended into Heaven with the promise that he would return, just as they had seen him go. His sacrificial death and resurrection means that all who believe in him can have eternal life.

The Resurrection Body

Paul's discourse on the resurrection, which occupies the whole of 1 Corinthinans 15, compares the resurrection of Jesus with the resurrection of believers at his return. Whether we are raised from the dead, or whether we are alive at the time of his coming, we will depart from this world to meet him. This event, known as the rapture, has already been mentioned in the context of the Jewish wedding customs, and we will discuss it in more detail later, but at this stage we need to look at Paul's explanation of a "mystery", that we shall all be changed, and become incorruptible and immortal.

> Behold, I show you a mystery; We shall not all sleep, but we shall all be changed, In a moment, in the twinkling of an eye, at the last trump: for the trumpet shall sound, and the dead shall be raised incorruptible, and we shall be changed. For this corruptible must put on incorruption, and this mortal must put on immortality. So when this corruptible shall have put on incorruption, and this mortal shall have put on immortality, then shall be brought to pass the saying that is written, Death is swallowed up in victory. O death, where is thy sting? O grave, where is thy victory?
>
> *1 Cor. 15:51-55*

We can easily understand what is meant by immortal. It means we will live for ever, as a consequence of rising from the dead, but what exactly does Paul mean when he says we will be "incorruptible"?

We might be inclined to think that he is referring to our spiritual state at the resurrection, that we will no longer be tainted by sin, and certainly this will be the case, but this is not what Paul means. He uses the Greek word *aphthartos*, which means indestructible, imperishable and incorruptible, and he associates it with *athanasia* which means immortality. It makes sense that these two words should appear together because there is no point being immortal, and no longer subject to the process of ageing and decay, if we are able to die in an accident. We have already discussed the immortality of Adam, before he sinned, and how he must have been indestructible. The same must apply to believers, after the rapture, otherwise we will spend eternity in a state of continual anxiety, taking care to avoid damaging ourselves. We will be immortal and physically indestructible, and we might have other strange properties that become apparent when we consider the resurrection body of Jesus.

Matthew's Gospel tells us that Mary Magdalene and the "other Mary" (the mother of Jesus)[16] came to the empty tomb, and the angel told them that Jesus had risen, and they should go to Galilee and tell the disciples. Jesus met the women while they were on their way, and they recognised him immediately and held him by the feet and worshipped him. Then he met the disciples in Galilee and when they saw him, they also worshipped him, but some doubted. Then he gave them the Great Commission to preach the Gospel to all the world, and by this time we have to assume that he had reassured them and resolved their doubts. The question is, what did they have doubts about? Did they fail to recognise him for some reason, or were they in such a state of shock, when they saw him risen from the dead, that they were unable to accept his obvious presence?

Mark's Gospel tells a similar story, except that it says he appeared first to Mary Magdalene, and she gave the news to "them that had been with him", which means some of the disciples, but they did not believe her. Then he appeared "in another form" to two of them as they went into the country. The question is, in what other form did he appear? Does this mean that Jesus was capable of changing his appearance? The two disciples believed that it was Jesus, and they went and told the others, but they did not believe. Then Jesus appeared to all eleven of them, and rebuked the nine

---

[16] Matt. 28.1. (c.f. 27:61). This Mary is the mother of James and Joses, (Matt. 27:56), the brothers of Jesus. (Matt. 13:55).

disciples who had not believed. Then he gave them the Great Commission, with some additional remarks about signs that would follow those that believe, and then he ascended into heaven.

We will skip over Luke's Gospel for the time being and discuss it later, because it has to be combined with the book of Acts, which was written by the same author and is a continuation of the story.

First we look at John's Gospel, where we are told that Mary Magdalene went to the tomb and found the stone moved away from the entrance, but it appears that she didn't go inside. Instead she went and told Simon Peter and "the other disciple whom Jesus loved", which means John himself, who wrote the Gospel. Peter and John ran to the tomb, but John ran faster and looked inside and saw the grave clothes. He didn't actually go inside. Instead it appears that he just stuck his head round the door. Then Peter arrived and went in and saw the linen clothes, and the napkin that was around his head wrapped up in a place by itself. Then John went in and saw everything, and believed, and then the two of them went home.

Then we have the story of Mary Magdalene returning to the tomb, and she stood outside weeping. She looked inside and there were two angels who asked her why she was weeping and she said *"Because they have taken away my Lord, and I know not where they have laid him"*. She thought the body of Jesus had been stolen. Then she turned round and saw Jesus, but she didn't recognise him, and thought he was the gardener. She wondered if he might have taken away the body, and asked him where he had put it. Then he said "Mary" and she recognised that it was Jesus, and said to him "Rabboni", which means "Master". Again, Jesus was recognised from his greeting, not from his appearance. Then he said *"Touch me not; for I am not yet ascended to my Father: but go to my brethren, and say unto them, I ascend unto my Father, and your Father; and to my God, and your God."* This does not mean that Jesus could not be touched before his ascension. We have already seen, from Matthew's Gospel, that the women held him by the feet, and we will soon see, from Luke's Gospel, that he invited the disciples to touch him. The Greek phrase *"me mou haptou"*, translated "Touch me not" is an imperative that means an action already in progress should be stopped, so literally it means "Stop touching me". It seems that Mary had given him a hug, which was a natural enough thing to do in the circumstances, and he wanted her to let go. He did not intend to remain in this world, and he did not want to be touched by a woman in a way that might cultivate false hopes, so he told her about his destination, that he would ascend to his Father. He also gave her some alternative work to do, that she should go and tell his brethren about his forthcoming ascension.

She went and told the disciples, according to his instructions, and then the same evening, he appeared to them in a room where the door was "shut" for fear of the Jews. Obviously this means "locked" or "bolted" because the purpose was to prevent the Jews from getting in. The news of the resurrection was likely to proliferate all sorts of rumours that the body of Jesus had been stolen, and the disciples would be blamed for it, and they were expecting persecution. Jesus appeared among them, as if the locked door presented no obstruction to him, and he said *"Peace be unto you"*. He showed them his hands and his side, and they were convinced that it was Jesus, and he commissioned them to preach the Gospel. This visit tells us something remarkable about the resurrection body of Jesus. He was capable of appearing out of absolutely nowhere, and he could pass through walls, or he could de-materialise from behind a wall and re-appear on the other side.

Then we have Thomas, who was not there when Jesus appeared and he would not believe that Jesus had risen until he had seen him, and touched the nail-prints in his hand and side. Eight days later, which means the following Sunday according to Jewish inclusive counting, the disciples were assembled again and the doors were "shut", which means they were locked, and Jesus appeared to them and greeted them in the same way, saying *"Peace be with you"*. This time, Thomas was able to touch the nail-prints in his hand and his side, and he believed.

Then Jesus appeared to the disciples again in Galilee, where they were fishing, but they had caught nothing. They saw Jesus standing on the shore, but they didn't recognise him. He told them to cast the net on the right side of the boat, and they did so, and they caught so many fish that they couldn't pull them all in. At this point, John recognised that it was Jesus, and said so to Peter. The other disciples brought another boat, and together they dragged the net to the shore. When they had finished, they saw that Jesus already had some fish, and was cooking it on a fire. He said to them *"Come and dine"*, and they all knew it was Jesus. He gave them bread and fish, and then he started his dialogue with Peter, saying *"Lovest thou me more than these?"* (meaning the fish). Peter was a fisherman by trade, as were the other disciples who came from Galilee, and they must have thought they were quite good at it. They would have been humiliated by a carpenter telling them how to catch fish, and then having his own fish, all cooked and ready to eat, by the time they got ashore. The point of the dialogue was, that if they loved Jesus and followed him, he could provide them with fish and everything else they needed. This was the third time he had revealed himself to them, after he had risen from the dead, and they had gone back to their fishing. Jesus was speaking personally to Peter, using the singular "thou" instead of the plural "you". (That's right, the King James English makes those distinctions). Jesus asked him the question three times and each time Peter answered *"Lord, thou knowest that I love thee"*. At this point, Peter was getting tired of being questioned, and he was getting jealous of John, who appeared to be the favourite disciple of Jesus. He suggested that John might be about to perform an act of betrayal, similar to Judas Iscariot. Not that a betrayal would mean anything, for Jesus in his resurrected body, because he was in the regular habit of appearing and disappearing at will. Jesus responded by saying *"If it be that he tarry till I come, what is that to thee? Follow thou me."* This was thought to mean that John would not die, but it wasn't meant that way. It was simply an instruction to Peter, to follow Jesus.

This appearance of Jesus at Galilee has the same characteristics as all the other appearances, that Jesus was recognised after he had said something or done something. They never recognised him while he was standing on the shore, but Peter recognised him when he had helped them to catch fish. Then they all recognised him when he said *"Come and dine"*.

Now we turn to Luke's Gospel, which tells us that the women returned from the tomb and told everything to the eleven, and to all the others, but nobody believed them. Peter found the linen clothes

41

in the tomb and wondered if it was true, but he wasn't sure. Then two of the disciples were on the road to Emmaus, and Jesus appeared to them, but they didn't recognise him. It says *"Their eyes were holden that they should not know him"*, which is a euphemism for lack of recognition and it doesn't mean there was something wrong with their eyes. They thought he was one of the many visitors who had gone to Jerusalem for the Passover. They were discussing the events of the last few days, and Jesus asked them why they were looking so sad, so they told him about the crucifixion, and the report from the women that he had risen, but they couldn't believe it. Then Jesus went through the Scriptures with them, beginning at Moses and going through all the prophets, telling them how Christ should suffer, and then be glorified. This must have been a lengthy discussion, but the disciples still did not recognise that this was Jesus. Then he spent the night with them, and while they were having dinner, he broke bread and they recognised him. It says their *"eyes were opened"*, which means they recognised him from the act of breaking bread, which must have been similar to the way he broke it on the night before he was crucified. Then, after he had broken bread, he vanished out of their sight. He didn't get up and go away, he simply vanished. This event, in Luke 24:31, cannot easily be compared with Luke 4:30, where Jesus was about to be thrown off a cliff, and it says *"he passing through the midst of them went his way"*. This is not a vanishing act. It seems more like he was walking through a group of people who were constrained from touching him, rather like the soldiers who fell over backwards when they came to arrest him at Gethsemane. (John 18:6). When he broke bread with the two disciples, after his resurrection, he vanished into nowhere, just as he was capable of appearing from nowhere, as we have seen from John's Gospel. Then the two disciples said to each other *"Did not our heart burn within us, while he talked with us by the way, and while he opened to us the scriptures?"* It's as if they felt rather silly, that they never recognised him from his conversation, even though it must have been the same as his conversation during his ministry. They never commented on his appearance, and this is a matter of significance, because if he had looked like the pre-resurrection Jesus, they would have said "Why didn't we recognise him?" Instead they commented on his conversation which bore a greater resemblance to the person they had known.

Then they returned to Jerusalem and told the eleven disciples and their companions. This means the two disciples were not part of the eleven, but were other followers of Jesus. They told what had happened to them on the road, and that Jesus had also appeared to Simon Peter. Then Jesus appeared among them and said *"Peace be unto you"*. Again, we have a sudden appearance from nowhere, and a familiar greeting that would help them to recognise him, but they were shocked and they thought they had seen a ghost. Some of them doubted that it was Jesus, and they doubted that it was a physical person at all, so he showed them his hands and his feet, and asked them to touch him. Then he ate some fish and honey in front of them to prove that he had appeared in a real, physical body. Then he went through the law of Moses with them, and the prophets, and showed how Christ should suffer and rise from the dead. The Gospel would be preached to all nations, and they were the witnesses to these things, but he asked them to stay in Jerusalem until they would be *"endued with power from on high"*. Then he took them to Bethany, which is a short distance from Jerusalem on the Mount of Olives, and he ascended into heaven. Then the disciples returned to Jerusalem, according to his instructions.

Now we turn to the book of Acts, which was written by Luke, and it's basically a continuation of Luke's Gospel, overlapping it slightly. In the first chapter of Acts, we read about how Jesus *"showed himself alive after his passion by many infallible proofs, being seen of them forty days"*. This explains why there are variant accounts of his appearances, because it implies that he appeared many times during those forty days. He told the disciples to remain in Jerusalem and wait for the baptism in the Holy Spirit, and they asked him *"Lord, wilt thou at this time restore again the kingdom to Israel?"* They must have been aware that Jesus had come in a body that was different from his pre-resurrection body. He could vanish at any time and re-appear somewhere else, and he could pass through walls and locked doors. Perhaps they thought that he had been endued with super-powers, so that he could make war against the Romans, and now he is promising the Holy Spirit to his disciples.

Perhaps they thought this is what was meant by *"power from on high"*. Can you imagine it? An army of invulnerable supermen could take on the Romans and liberate Israel. Jesus did not entirely deny their request. He told them *"It is not for you to know the times or the seasons, which the Father hath put in his own power"*. In other words, he was saying something like, "All in good time, but not now". Then he told them the purpose for which they would receive power. It was so that they could preach the Gospel to all the world. Then he ascended into heaven and a cloud took him out of their sight. Two angels said to them *"Why stand ye gazing up into heaven? This same Jesus, which is taken up from you into heaven, shall so come in like manner as ye have seen him go into heaven."* Perhaps they thought they were supposed to ascend with him, or perhaps they imagined that if they gazed long enough they might see a glimpse of him. In reality, the message of the angels was "Get on with it, there is work to do". Then they returned to Jerusalem from the Mount of Olives. The rest of the story is about the appointment of someone to replace Judas Iscariot, then the day of Pentecost and the birth of the church, followed by the ministry of the church and the journeys of the Apostle Paul.

Having come to the end of our commentary on the Gospels and the book of Acts, we return to the following remarks from Paul:

> There is one glory of the sun, and another glory of the moon, and another glory of the stars: for one star differeth from another star in glory. So also is the resurrection of the dead. It is sown in corruption; it is raised in incorruption: It is sown in dishonour; it is raised in glory: it is sown in weakness; it is raised in power: It is sown a natural body; it is raised a spiritual body. There is a natural body, and there is a spiritual body. And so it is written, The first man Adam was made a living soul; the last Adam was made a quickening spirit. Howbeit that was not first which is spiritual, but that which is natural; and afterward that which is spiritual. The first man is of the earth, earthy: the second man is the Lord from heaven.
>
> *1 Cor. 15:41-47*

Clearly, Paul was referring to the body of Jesus, after his resurrection, as a "spiritual body", and this is a status that we will attain at the rapture. A spiritual body is not pure spirit, and Jesus was not a ghost. He had physical properties, but he was not subject to physical laws and could move in a realm that was outside of the domain in which we live. Paul says that there is more than one type of spiritual body, just as there are the sun, moon and different types of stars. We have seen, from the resurrection body of Jesus, a brief glimpse of what a spiritual body might be like, and we will find out, at his coming, what sort of bodies we will inherit.

We see that Adam was made of the earth, as a living soul, and Paul's discussion of him seems to be limited to his fallen state, otherwise there would be no need for a "quickening spirit". We can only wonder at what type of body Adam might have had, before he took the forbidden fruit, but we can be sure that, at the very least, he must have been indestructible, because this is an essential property that goes with immortality.

The Church Age

Now we live in the Church Age, when the Gospel is being preached to all the world, according the Great Commission:

> And Jesus came and spake unto them, saying, All power is given unto me in heaven and in earth. Go ye therefore, and teach all nations, baptizing them in the name of the Father, and of the Son, and of the Holy Ghost: Teaching them to observe all things whatsoever I have commanded you: and, lo, I am with you alway, even unto the end of the world.[17] Amen.
>
> *Matt. 28:18-20*

Since that time, the Gospel has continued to be preached, and those who believe are restored to a relationship with God which means:

- We are free from the penalty of sin. Jesus has paid the price of all our sins once and for all on the cross, so that we can be forgiven.
- We are in the process of being set free from the power of sin, as we learn how to live in fellowship with God.

---

[17] The Greek *aeon* means "age".

- We have the promise that one day we will be set free from the presence of sin. We continue to live in our mortal bodies and will die physically, but we will rise to eternal life when Jesus returns, and will accompany him during the fulfilment of other prophetic events.

The concept of "eternal life" means all three of these things. There is a tendency among some Evangelicals today to emphasise the first two, with a promise that fellowship with God extends beyond the grave in a spiritual place called "heaven", but the early church was much more specific. They believed in an immediate after-life where they would enjoy the Lord's presence (2 Cor. 5:8; Phil. 1:23), but it was not their final destination. Instead, they emphasised that they would rise from the dead, just as Jesus had risen from the dead.

Since the days of the early church, the Gospel has been preached with varying degrees of effectiveness. In Revelation 2 and 3, John wrote about the seven churches, showing how most of them had gone off the rails in some way. During the Middle Ages, the church in Western Europe had gone astray even further, and had become a powerful political force with its centre in Rome. It became rich by giving people the promise of heaven by paying indulgences. Then there was the Reformation which stripped the Roman Catholic Church of its political power, and restored the true Gospel of salvation by faith in Jesus Christ.

Wherever the true Gospel is preached, it brings persecution, and this is true today, just as it was in the early church. In the former Soviet Union, Christians were allowed to meet in official state-controlled churches under heavily restricted conditions, and those who were not satisfied with it would meet in secret, at risk of being arrested and taken away to prisons or work camps. Now the greatest threat is from Islam, where Christians live in fear of attack from their Muslim neighbours who can act with impunity because of a system of Shari'a law that is biased in favour of Muslims. In some countries, Christians are not allowed to build new churches, or even to repair existing churches. If they attempt to carry out repairs quietly, without asking permission, they risk persecution from the state.

On the face of it, much of the persecution against Christians seems totally irrational, and nation states will attempt to deny that it exists. In the Soviet Union they used to have "show churches" where foreign visitors could be invited so that they could see how much religious freedom there was, when in fact there was no freedom at all.

Why should the Gospel be considered such a threat? The reason is that the serpent continues to exercise his power on the earth. When Jesus died on the cross, he said *"It is finished"* meaning he had paid the price of our redemption, then he rose again to show that he had conquered death. However, the battle against the serpent was not yet finished. The Messiah had been bruised in the heel, but the serpent's head is not yet crushed. Now the serpent's fury rages against the servants of the Messiah, and we have to participate in the battle, until the Messiah comes again and finishes him off.

> And there appeared a great wonder in heaven; a woman clothed with the sun, and the moon under her feet, and upon her head a crown of twelve stars: And she being with child cried, travailing in birth, and pained to be delivered. And there appeared another wonder in heaven; and behold a great red dragon, having seven heads and ten horns, and seven crowns upon his heads ... And when the dragon saw that he was cast unto the earth, he persecuted the woman which brought forth the man child. And to the woman were given two wings of a great eagle, that she might fly into the wilderness, into her place, where she is nourished for a time, and times, and half a time, from the face of the serpent. And the serpent cast out of his mouth water as a flood after the woman, that he might cause her to be carried away of the flood. And the earth helped the woman, and the earth opened her mouth, and swallowed up the flood which the dragon cast out of his mouth. And the dragon was wroth with the woman, and went to make war with the remnant of her seed, which keep the commandments of God, and have the testimony of Jesus Christ.
>
> *Rev. 12:1-17*

This passage describes the flight of Israel from a future world dictator called the Antichrist, for a period of three and a half years, described here as *"a time, and times, and half a time"*. The twelve stars represent the twelve tribes of Israel, by comparison with Joseph's dream (Gen. 37:9). However, the passage has a double meaning, and it also refers to Herod's soldiers arriving in Bethlehem when Jesus was an infant, killing all the male children up to two years old in an attempt to kill Jesus. But God had warned Joseph, to whom Mary was betrothed, and they went off quickly to Egypt with the infant Jesus before Herod's men arrived. Then they returned sometime later, after the death of Herod, and Jesus grew up in Nazareth and eventually began his ministry.

Clearly this was an attempt by the serpent to prevent the ministry of Jesus from taking place, and a similar event occurred at the time of Moses, when Pharaoh ordered that the midwives should kill the Hebrew male children at birth. The midwives refused and made the excuse that the Hebrew women gave birth too quickly, before they could get there. Then Pharaoh ordered that the male children should be thrown into the river. Moses was put into a waterproof basket and placed among the reeds, where he was saved by Pharaoh's daughter, and he grew up, and eventually he led the Israelites out of Egypt. So we see that the serpent carried out acts of infanticide, both at the time of Moses and Jesus, to prevent God's purposes from being achieved, but in both cases his attempts failed. Jesus completed his work, and now the serpent rages against his followers who preach the Gospel.

The Church in Transition

The entire period of the Church, from the time when it was formed on the day of Pentecost, until the time when Jesus returns, represents a transition state comparable to the period of betrothal of a Jewish bride. The price of redemption has been paid, and the bride waits for her husband to come and take her away unexpectedly during the night, to the place that he has prepared for her in his father's house.

The Apostle Paul speaks of the church in a transition state on a number occasions. In his first letter to the Corinthians he spoke of spiritual gifts, and then he extolled charity, which means love, as the greatest virtue that will remain, together with faith and hope, when spiritual gifts have vanished.

> Though I speak with the tongues of men and of angels, and have not charity, I am become as sounding brass, or a tinkling cymbal ... Charity

never faileth: but whether there be prophecies, they shall fail; whether there be tongues, they shall cease; whether there be knowledge, it shall vanish away. For we know in part, and we prophesy in part. But when that which is perfect is come, then that which is in part shall be done away. When I was a child, I spake as a child, I understood as a child, I thought as a child: but when I became a man, I put away childish things. For now we see through a glass, darkly; but then face to face: now I know in part; but then shall I know even as also I am known. And now abideth faith, hope, charity, these three; but the greatest of these is charity.

1 Cor. 13:1-13

His remark that *"we see through a glass, darkly; but then face to face"* can only be a reference to the coming of the Messiah. When the bride gets up in the night to go with her husband, she puts on a nice dress (if she isn't wearing it already) and she takes her lamp, and a few clothes for the time she will spend in her bridegroom's chamber, and she leaves everything else behind. This is the moment she has waited for, and she is only concerned about her husband, so the quality she takes with her is *love*.

She might not have known him very well up to that point, and it's likely that the rest of her family knows him better than she does. While waiting for him to come, she must have wondered many times, "What is he really like?", but now she is going to know him in a way that nobody else can know.

At a later date, when persecution was getting worse, Paul wrote to the church in Rome as follows:

For I reckon that the sufferings of this present time are not worthy to be compared with the glory which shall be revealed in us. For the earnest expectation of the creation waiteth for the revelation of the sons of God[18] ... For we know that the whole creation groaneth and travaileth in pain together until now.

Rom. 8:18-22

---

[18] For purposes of clarity, this is a modification of the KJAV. The actual text says: *For the earnest expectation of the creature waiteth for the manifestation of the sons of God.*

As persecution got worse, at the time of Nero, the early Christians had all the more reason to hope for the return of Messiah, but this was always their constant theme, even in times of peace. They lived at a time when the Gospel spread rapidly throughout the Greek and Roman world, and they might have felt pleased about their achievements, but they were always looking forward to another world that would be much better than this one, where even the creation itself would be liberated, as the effects of the fall are reversed.

The early Christians lived in the expectation that Jesus would come soon, although they must have known that before he comes, there is a job that needs to be finished.

> And this gospel of the kingdom shall be preached in all the world for a witness unto all nations; and then shall the end come.
>
> *Matt. 24:14*

If the Gospel had been preached for a few more centuries, as it had been during the first century, it would have easily reached all the world, but the church has had many failures and I have mentioned a few of them on page 46.

However, if we look at the whole timescale since creation and the fall, we should not be surprised that the return of Messiah is taking a long time. The Protevangelic prophecy was given immediately after the fall, and Jesus did not appear on the scene until 4000 years later. In the Jewish wedding scenario, this represents the interval between the time when the father first thought of finding a bride for his son, and the contract being offered. In that context, the period of 2000 years that Christ has been betrothed to his church does not seem all that long. We might have to wait a long time yet, but we have to be ready, whenever he comes.

Interpretation of Prophecy

From this point onwards, up to the end of this chapter, we will discuss topics that have caused much debate among theologians, about the end-time events and the order in which they occur. The sequence of events has to be established by stitching together various prophecies and visions that occur in different parts of the Bible, so that they come together as a coherent whole. The prophecies are rather like the parables of Jesus, given to us in such a way that they are revealed to those who diligently seek the truth, and hidden from the rest of the world.

Isaac Newton[19] took the view that many prophecies have already been fulfilled, and they can be understood in great detail, and as examples he gives the four empires predicted by Daniel, namely the Babylonians, Medo-Persians, Greeks and Romans. He said that futuristic prophecy is more obscure, but would become clear as the time for their fulfilment approaches.

There are many books on Bible prophecy today, and I have not yet found one that I would entirely agree with, but I would recommend the work of Arnold Fruchtenbaum[20] and Allan Cundick.[21]

Return of the Messiah

There are actually two second comings of Christ. First he comes *for* his saints, to take them out of the world, then he comes *with* his saints, to cleanse the earth and establish his kingdom.

The coming of Christ *for* his saints is as follows:

> But I would not have you to be ignorant, brethren, concerning them which are asleep, that ye sorrow not, even as others which have no hope. For if we believe that Jesus died and rose again, even so them also which sleep in Jesus will God bring with him. For this we say unto you by the word of the Lord, that we which are alive and remain unto the coming of the Lord shall not prevent them which are asleep. For the Lord himself shall descend from heaven with a shout, with the voice of the archangel, and with the trump of God: and the dead in Christ shall rise first: Then we which are alive and remain shall be caught up together with them in the clouds, to meet the Lord in the air: and so shall we ever be with the Lord. Wherefore comfort one another with these words.
>
> *1 Thess. 4:13 -18*

---

[19] Manuel, Frank, *Isaac Newton: Historian*, chap. 9, *History Sacred and Profane Connected*.

[20] Fruchtenbaum, Arnold, *The Footsteps of the Messiah*.

[21] Cundick, Allan, *The Divine Revelation of the Future*.

This event is the "rapture", already mentioned on pages 29 and 37, and we have seen how we will be raised incorruptible (or indestructible) and immortal (1 Cor. 15:51-55). It will be a time of great celebration for believers, but those left on earth will witness the arrival of a world dictator known as the Antichrist. His Biblical name is derived from the Greek word *ante* which means "substitute", so he is a false Messiah. He will make a seven-year covenant with the existing political authorities which have merged into a world government, and they will be allowed to continue, subject to his overall rule. He will also allow religious observance to continue, under the supervision of a one-world interfaith movement described as the "mother of harlots" (Rev. 17:5). During that time, sacrifices will be offered at the Temple in Jerusalem, and for this to take place, the Temple has to be rebuilt. Of course this requires the return of the Jewish people to Israel, a condition that has already been accomplished in recent history.

After three and a half years he will break his covenant and declare himself to be in total control, abolishing all other forms of government. He will require that everyone will have to take his mark of allegiance on the right hand or forehead. He will even declare himself to be God, and will set up an image of himself in the Temple, known as the "abomination of the desolation". At the same time, he will abolish all other religions.

He is able to achieve all this because he is no ordinary human. He is part of a demonic trinity with Satan as the father, himself as the son, and another entity called the "false prophet" as the demonic counterpart of the Holy Spirit. The Antichrist gets assassinated, but he rises from the dead, so there is a demonic resurrection which increases his power. The Antichrist is otherwise known as the "beast" and he is supported by the false prophet who is known as "another beast" (Rev. 13:11). The false prophet gives power to the Antichrist by working miracles in his presence.

The reign of the Antichrist, during this seven-year period, is known as the tribulation. It gets particularly nasty after the mid-point when he breaks his covenant, because anyone who refuses to take his mark of allegiance will not be able to buy or sell, and anyone who refuses to worship his image will be killed.

The seven-year reign of Antichrist, divided into two parts, is derived from a passage in Daniel's prophecy where a "week" means a week of years.

> ... the people of the prince that shall come shall destroy the city and the sanctuary; and the end thereof shall be with a flood, and unto the end of the war desolations are determined. And he shall confirm the covenant with many for one week: and in the midst of the week he shall cause the sacrifice and the oblation to cease, and for the overspreading of abominations he shall make it desolate, even until the consummation, and that determined shall be poured upon the desolate.
>
> *Dan. 9:26-27*

There is a theological discussion about whether the believers will be raptured at the beginning of the seven-year reign of Antichrist, or at the mid-point when the tribulation begins, or at the end of the tribulation. These views are called *pre-trib, mid-trib* and *post-trib*. Historically, Christians have always had to endure persecution, and we shouldn't expect to get an early exit just to have an easy time, but there are a number of reasons why the pre-tribulation rapture must be correct:

• There are a number of Bible passages that describe how the believers will be removed, in advance of a future time of trial. See, for example Luke 21:36; 1 Thess. 1:10; Rev. 3:10.

• The pre-tribulation rapture fits in most easily with the Jewish wedding customs, where the bride and groom remain in their chamber, shut away from the world until the seventh day, when they come out and join the other guests. This seven-day period corresponds to the seven-year reign of the Antichrist.

• The pre-tribulation rapture is the only scenario that involves an effective element of surprise. Just as the groom surprises his bride when he comes for her during the night, so the Lord will come and surprise his church. Jesus taught emphatically that we will not know the time of his coming. (Matt. 24:36-44; Luke 12:40; 1 Thess. 5:2; Rev. 16:15). The rapture cannot be at the mid-point of the tribulation, because it would be possible to calculate the timing exactly, by counting three and a half years from the time when the Antichrist makes his seven-year covenant. Neither can it be after the tribulation, because it would have to be squeezed in somewhere, between the end of the tribulation and the beginning of the millennium.

- In Bible passages that describe the tribulation, the church is always absent. The most notable example is the Book of Revelation, where the first three chapters are about the seven churches of Asia Minor, and then the church disappears and is not mentioned again until she re-appears as the bride of Christ. Chapters 4 to 18 are about the tribulation, then in chapter 19 we have the Marriage of the Lamb and the return of Christ to the earth *with* his saints who are described as the armies in heaven. Chapter 20 describes the millennium and the Great White Throne Judgement, then in chapter 21 there is the New Heaven and the New Earth, and the bride appears symbolically as the New Jerusalem. In that case, the church must have been raptured between chapters 3 and 4, and after that she is known only as the bride.

- Revelation 7 describes a group of tribulation saints who are different from the church saints, so they must have appeared later, after the church has gone. We will deal with this question soon, when we discuss the situation of those who are left behind after the rapture, but first we will make a small digression.

There is an observation that needs to be made about the seven churches of Asia Minor, described in the first three chapters of Revelation. Although it appears that John was writing about the situation of the churches in his own time, these descriptions are arranged in a sequence that corresponds to the entire history of the church, up to the present time.[22]

---

[22] For a detailed description of how the seven churches of Asia Minor correspond to the entire church history, see Arnold Fruchtenbaum's *Footsteps of the Messiah*.

- The church of Ephesus represents the second generation believers in the early church who had lost their first love. They did not have the enthusiasm of the original founders of their churches.

- The church of Smyrna represents the period of persecution under the Romans.

- The church at Pergamos represents the church that became allied to the state, from the time of Constantine in AD 313.

- The church at Thyatira represents the period known as the dark ages, from about AD 600 when the Roman Catholic church dominated the religious life of Europe and taught a variety of false doctrines such as transubstantiation (the transformation of the bread and wine into the real body and blood of Jesus) and indulgences (paying money to get your friends and family out of purgatory).

- The church at Sardis represents the Reformation, beginning in 1517 when Martin Luther nailed his 95 Articles to his church door. He emphasised that salvation was personal, not dependent on the church, and Bible translations were made available so that people could read it for themselves. This brought a revival of pure doctrine, but the church was still allied to the state, with the Lutheran church in Germany and the Anglican church in England. They had a name for being alive, but were dead.

- The church at Philadelphia represents the great missionary movement that lasted from about 1700 to 1900. During that time there was hardly a place in the world where missionaries could not go, and this is represented by the open door that no man can shut.

- The church at Laodicea represents the descent into apostasy that has characterised the church from about 1900 to the present time. This is a lukewarm church, ruled entirely by men, and Jesus is not even there. Instead he is outside, knocking on the door, waiting to get in.

Considering that church history has progressed through this entire sequence, and we are now in the age of the Laodicean church, the question arises, "What happens next?" The church disappears from the Book of Revelation at this point, so are we heading for the Rapture? Nobody knows when it will happen, but the most important question is, "Are you ready?"

Now we come to the end of this digression and return to our purpose. Those who believe in Jesus (including some who have given up on all forms of organised church because of the apostasy), will rise and meet Jesus when he comes. What will happen to those who are left behind? It will be a complete disaster, even without the appearance of the Antichrist, especially for people who are travelling. All the motorways will be gridlocked and strewn with wreckage as drivers disappear, leaving their vehicles to crash, together with their helpless passengers. Aircraft will crash as pilots and air traffic controllers disappear. Those who are at home, or not travelling anywhere, will escape the carnage but will face power cuts and shortage of food in the shops. There will be political turmoil as people try to rationalise the sudden disappearance of so many people from the face of the earth. Some people will say that some kind of secret weapon has been deployed. Others will say that it's an alien abduction on a massive scale.

Others, who are wiser, will realise that this is the event called the Rapture, that their Christian friends used to talk about. They will wonder "Why didn't I believe, and do I have a second chance?" The answer is yes, they do have a second chance, because the Bible talks about a group of believers who have gone through the "great tribulation".

> And one of the elders answered, saying unto me, What are these which are arrayed in white robes? and whence came they? And I said unto him, Sir, thou knowest. And he said to me, These are they which came out of great tribulation, and have washed their robes, and made them white in the blood of the Lamb.
>
> *Rev. 7:13-14*

These people must be different from other believers, because they are introduced in a way that makes them look like gate-crashers at a party, as if nobody knows who they are. They are different because they have endured the tribulation, while other believers have escaped it. The rapture has to occur before the tribulation, otherwise these believers would be part of the church and there would be nothing different about them, and this answers the question about the tribulation saints that was raised on page 54.

There will be a time of spiritual renewal during the tribulation, primarily due to the preaching of 144,000 Jewish believers, from the twelve tribes of Israel. These are mentioned in Revelation 7, together with the fruit of their labour, the tribulation saints who are a great multitude beyond number, taken from all the nations (which means the Gentiles). Salvation will still be available, to all who believe, but they will have to make up their minds quickly. When the mid-point of the tribulation period is reached, and the Antichrist makes his demand that everyone should worship his image, and take his mark, this will be the final opportunity to decide between Christ and Antichrist. The following passage describes the demands of the false prophet who represents the Antichrist and works miracles on his behalf:

> And he had power to give life unto the image of the beast, that the image of the beast should both speak, and cause that as many as would not worship the image of the beast should be killed. And he causeth all, both small and great, rich and poor, free and bond, to receive a mark in their right hand, or in their foreheads: And that no man might buy or sell, save he that had the mark, or the name of the beast, or the number of his name.
>
> *Rev. 13:15-17*

While this might seem a bit stiff, the demands of Christ are much more severe:

> And the third angel followed them, saying with a loud voice, If any man worship the beast and his image, and receive his mark in his forehead, or in his hand, the same shall drink of the wine of the wrath of God, which is poured out without mixture into the cup of his indignation; and he shall be tormented with fire and brimstone in the presence of the holy angels, and in the presence of the Lamb: And the

> smoke of their torment ascendeth up for ever and ever: and they have
> no rest day nor night, who worship the beast and his image, and
> whosoever receiveth the mark of his name.
>
> *Rev. 14:9-11*

There is only one realistic choice that can be made, because when
people take the mark of the beast, they have reached the point of no
return when salvation is no longer available. It is much better to
follow Christ and take the risk of getting killed by the Antichrist,
than to reach the point of no return with God. Many people will wish
that they had believed before the rapture so that they would never
have to face this choice. Others will carelessly take the line of least
resistance, apparently unconcerned that millions have already
disappeared from the world in an event that was prophesied in
advance, and the remaining prophecies will come true. People will
make their choice, one way or the other, and those who foolishly
choose to follow the Antichrist will benefit from only short-term
gain. The Antichrist will pursue the saints and kill many of them, but
not all of them. Some will escape and survive until the end of his
reign, including those of Israel, already mentioned on page 47, who
are typified as the woman with the crown of twelve stars. While the
massacre continues, the souls of the martyrs will cry to the Lord as
follows:

> And when he had opened the fifth seal, I saw under the altar the souls
> of them that were slain for the word of God, and for the testimony
> which they held: And they cried with a loud voice, saying, How long,
> O Lord, holy and true, dost thou not judge and avenge our blood on
> them that dwell on the earth? And white robes were given unto every
> one of them; and it was said unto them, that they should rest yet for a
> little season, until their fellowservants also and their brethren, that
> should be killed as they were, should be fulfilled.
>
> *Rev. 6:9-11*

The "little season" is the time remaining until the three and a half
years are finished, and the Lord returns with his saints who were
taken away during the rapture, and he overthrows the Antichrist. The
end-time events are discussed in detail in the last four chapters of

Revelation, but the dramatic return of the Lord is recorded briefly in a much more ancient passage.

> And Enoch also, the seventh from Adam, prophesied of these, saying, Behold, the Lord cometh with ten thousands of his saints, to execute judgement upon all, and to convince all that are ungodly among them of all their ungodly deeds which they have ungodly committed, and of all their hard speeches which ungodly sinners have spoken against him.
>
> *Jude 14-15*

This passage is a quotation from the Book of Enoch,[23] which is thought to be a collection of fragments from various sources, but Jude obviously believes that this fragment comes from Enoch, the seventh from Adam who was translated to heaven and never died.

To continue the story, we need to turn the clock back a little and look at the situation of the saints who have been raptured. While there has been complete mayhem on earth, under the reign of the Antichrist, the saints have been celebrating a wedding in heaven. For most of the time, there has just been the bride and groom together, but as they approach the time of his return, there is the marriage supper, where a large number of guests are invited.

> Let us be glad and rejoice, and give honour to him: for the marriage of the Lamb is come, and his wife hath made herself ready. And to her was granted that she should be arrayed in fine linen, clean and white: for the fine linen is the righteousness of saints. And he saith unto me, Write, Blessed are they which are called unto the marriage supper of the Lamb. And he saith unto me, These are the true sayings of God.
>
> *Rev. 19:7-9*

The bride is the church, and the guests at the marriage supper are the Old Testament saints and possibly also the tribulation saints. We have already seen, on page 51, that the rapture happens in two stages. The dead in Christ will rise first, then those who are alive and remain shall be caught up and meet the Lord in the air. If the Old

---

[23] Charles, R.H. *The Book of Enoch*, p.32.

Testament saints and tribulation saints are to join them for the marriage supper, at the end of the seven year period, there has to be additional resurrections. The following passage affirms that multiple resurrections do occur, each in their own order.

> For as in Adam all die, even so in Christ shall all be made alive. But every man in his own order: Christ the firstfruits; afterward they that are Christ's at his coming.
>
> *1 Cor. 15:22-23*

The remainder of Revelation tells us what happens after the wedding. Jesus comes as the rider on the white horse, clothed with a vesture dipped in blood which is the price he has paid for his bride. He defeats the beast (the Antichrist) and the false prophet, and throws them into the lake of fire. (Rev.19:11-21). He slaughters the armies of the Antichrist, and the remnant of his followers who have taken his mark, and they wait for the resurrection of unbelievers at the Final Judgement. Then he takes hold of the serpent, known as the Devil and Satan, and throws him into the bottomless pit where he remains for a thousand years. (Rev. 20:1-3). Then we have a passage that describes the status of the saints who accompany the Messiah.

> And I saw thrones, and they sat upon them, and judgment was given unto them: and I saw the souls of them that were beheaded for the witness of Jesus, and for the word of God, and which had not worshipped the beast, neither his image, neither had received his mark upon their foreheads, or in their hands; and they lived and reigned with Christ a thousand years. But the rest of the dead lived not again until the thousand years were finished. This is the first resurrection. Blessed and holy is he that hath part in the first resurrection: on such the second death hath no power, but they shall be priests of God and of Christ, and shall reign with him a thousand years.
>
> *Rev. 20:4-6*

This passage describes all the resurrected saints, including the church saints, the Old Testament saints, and the tribulation saints who are identified by their refusal to take the mark of the beast. It cannot be ascertained for certain whether or not the tribulation saints were raptured and joined the Messiah and his bride for the marriage supper, but we see that they are present with him after he has returned to earth, so they must have been resurrected.

The *"first resurrection"* is a generic term that includes all the resurrections of the saints, in whatever order they might occur, and it protects us from the *"second death"*, which is the fate of unbelievers who are resurrected later, for the Final Judgement.

We have already seen, on page 18, that Daniel wrote about how the dead will rise, some to everlasting life, and some to shame and everlasting contempt. Taken alone, this would imply a single resurrection and judgement, but Daniel does not say so specifically. The books of Daniel and Revelation are complementary. Daniel speaks of the resurrection in general terms, and Revelation tells us how it will happen, not all at once, but in stages.

John, the author of Revelation, is also the author of John's Gospel, where he writes about the resurrection as follows:

> Verily, verily, I say unto you, The hour is coming, and now is, when the dead shall hear the voice of the Son of God: and they that hear shall live. For as the Father hath life in himself; so hath he given to the Son to have life in himself; And hath given him authority to execute judgment also, because he is the Son of man. Marvel not at this: for the hour is coming, in the which all that are in the graves shall hear his voice, And shall come forth; they that have done good, unto the resurrection of life; and they that have done evil, unto the resurrection of damnation.
>
> *John 5:25-29*

This passage, like the passage in Daniel, does not give any specific order of events, but it refers to the *"resurrection of life"* and the *"resurrection of damnation"* as if there are two resurrections. There are in fact two categories of resurrection. The resurrection of life, otherwise known as the "first resurrection" occurs in multiple stages, and then the resurrection of damnation occurs all at once before the Final Judgement.

Those who take part in the first resurrection will rule and reign with Christ for a thousand years, in the period that is known as the millennium. During this period, the world will be in a state of near perfection where evil will be restrained and there will be a partial restoration of the conditions that existed in the Garden of Eden before the fall.

Those who enter the millennium as resurrected saints will be immortal and will continue through the entire period and enter the next phase which is the New Heaven and New Earth. The remainder of the population will consist of those who refused the mark of the beast and survived the tribulation. They have not been resurrected, and from that point of view there is no reason to believe that they are immortal, although there is no mention of the death of believers during the millennium. At the very least, they will have great longevity, described in the following passage:

> There shall be no more thence an infant of days, nor an old man that hath not filled his days: for the child shall die an hundred years old; but the sinner being an hundred years old shall be accursed.
>
> *Isaiah 65:20*

During the millennium, anyone who dies at the age of 100 will be considered to have died young. The passage also suggests that the length of a person's life will depend on their spiritual state, and in that case who are the unbelievers who die young? They cannot be the resurrected saints, or the saints who have refused the mark of the beast. They can only be the children, born during the millennium, who are given the choice to believe or disbelieve, the same as anybody else. There are some who say that death during the millennium is for unbelievers only,[24] on the basis that the first resurrection is completed with the resurrection of the tribulation saints. (Rev. 20:4-6, see page 60). However, this is a derived result, rather than an explicit statement, and we will know with greater certainty as the events unfold.

During the millennium, the animals will be at peace, as they were in the Garden of Eden. They will no longer kill each other for food and will return to a vegetarian diet:

---

[24] See, for example, Arnold Fruchtenbaum's *Footsteps of the Messiah*, Chapter 17, *General Characteristics of the Messianic Kingdom*.

The wolf will live with the lamb, and the leopard will lie down with the young goat; The calf, the young lion, and the fattened calf together; and a little child will lead them. The cow and the bear will graze. Their young ones will lie down together. The lion will eat straw like the ox. The nursing child will play near a cobra's hole, and the weaned child will put his hand on the viper's den. They will not hurt nor destroy in all my holy mountain; for the earth will be full of the knowledge of Yahweh, as the waters cover the sea.

Isaiah 11:6-9, World English Bible

There will be a form of government during the millennium, in which Jesus the Messiah rules over the whole world, and his resurrected saints rule with him. They will live in a place called the *"camp of the saints"* and the *"beloved city"*, which means Jerusalem. At the end of the millennium, the serpent is released from his pit and deceives the nations, and goes to war against the saints. This is a futile activity, if ever there was one, and nobody would undertake such a venture unless they were truly deceived. The saints have already been resurrected, in their immortal, indestructible bodies, and the nations who are mortal are going to war against them. Perhaps when the serpent comes out of his pit, he will consider it to be a resurrection of some sort, and he will try to give immortality to his followers, but he has no such power. The saints could have defeated these armies easily, but they are not required to stain their hands with blood. Instead, fire comes down from God out of heaven, and devours the serpent and his armies, and throws them into the lake of fire, where they will join the beast and false prophet, and be tormented day and night for ever and ever. (Rev. 20:6-10).

The Messiah was bruised in the heel, when he was crucified, but now the serpent has been bruised in the head, so we have the complete fulfilment of the Protevangelic prophecy that was given as soon as Adam and Eve had sinned.

Then we come to the Final Judgement, where all the dead are raised, who have not been raised already.

And I saw a great white throne, and him that sat on it, from whose face the earth and the heaven fled away; and there was found no place for them. And I saw the dead, small and great, stand before God; and the

books were opened: and another book was opened, which is the book
of life: and the dead were judged out of those things which were
written in the books, according to their works. And the sea gave up the
dead which were in it; and death and hell delivered up the dead which
were in them: and they were judged every man according to their
works. And death and hell were cast into the lake of fire. This is the
second death. And whosoever was not found written in the book of life
was cast into the lake of fire.

Rev. 20:11-15

This is the judgement of all the unbelievers who have ever lived
since the beginning of the world, including those who died during
the millennium. If there is no death of believers during the
millennium, it means all those present at this judgement will be
unbelievers. The book of life is opened, but there is no mention of
anyone's name being found there, and we are only told what happens
to those whose names are not found. In that case, the book of life is
there, not to offer hope to anyone, but to show that it does not
include their names.

After the Final Judgement, the Lord creates a New Heaven and a
New Earth, and the New Jerusalem comes down from Heaven as a
bride adorned for her husband. This is a symbolic representation of
the bride as the New Jerusalem, and emphasises that she is
inseparable from the city, which is her eternal dwelling place. The
bride herself, which is the church, was already married to the
Messiah a thousand years earlier. There is a description of the city,
with twelve gates bearing the names of the twelve apostles. There is
no temple, and no need for a sun and moon, because the Lord God
and the Lamb are the temple, and they provide light for the city.

The city is finally identified as a restored paradise, where the
water of life flows out of the throne of God and of the Lamb, and in
the middle of the street there is the Tree of Life, which means the
inhabitants of the city will be immortal. There will be *no more curse*,
meaning the curse that was placed on Adam and Eve, because of
their sin, will be totally cancelled. The millennium was a partial
restoration of the conditions that existed before the fall, but in the
New Jerusalem the restoration will be total.

All Together in the End

I have attempted to describe the rapture, the tribulation, the millennium, the New Heaven and New Earth, and the associated prophetic events in a way that makes the most sense. There are various interpretations of prophecy, and people might try to arrange the sequence of events in a different order, but inevitably they all end up in the same place. The Bible starts off in Genesis with two immortal humans in the Garden of Eden, enjoying perfect fellowship with God, and it ends in Revelation where we have the saints of God, enjoying immortality and perfect fellowship with God, in a restored paradise called the New Jerusalem.

Summary of the Real Gospel

The Real Gospel (as opposed to the Pseudo-Gospel that I will describe later) consists of the following essential components:

- God created the world in a state of perfection. Adam and Eve were immortal, knowing nothing of sin.

- The woman, enticed by the serpent, took the forbidden fruit from the tree of knowledge of good and evil, and ate it so that she fell. Then she gave it to her husband, and he ate it, so he also fell. They were thrown out of the Garden of Eden, so that they died spiritually, but were given limited access to God by offering sacrifices (as we can see from the story of their first two sons, Cain and Abel). They were also placed under a sentence of physical death and were told they would return to the dust from which they came. The tree of life still existed in the garden, but they were prevented from accessing it, in case they might live for ever in their sinful state and multiply one evil upon another.

- They were given the Protevangelic prophecy, saying that a Messiah, born of a virgin, would come and defeat the serpent, but in the process he would receive an injury.

- After a long history which involved the Flood and the re-population of the world, then the nation of Israel and the law of Moses, finally Jesus the Messiah came. He was fully human, but not under the curse of sin as we are, and he offered himself as the perfect sacrifice, paying the price of our sin, then he rose from the dead to show that death had not overcome him. His sacrificial death and resurrection means that all who believe in him can have eternal life. He appeared to his disciples on a number of occasions, then he ascended into Heaven with the promise that he would return, just as they had seen him go.

- We now live in the church age, when the Gospel is being preached to the world, and those who believe are restored to spiritual life and communion with God. We continue to live in our mortal bodies and will die physically, but death has no sting and we know that our communion with God continues beyond the grave.

- When Jesus returns, the dead who have believed in him will rise to eternal life. Those who are alive at his coming will also rise and meet him in the air, and we will be forever with the Lord, with transformed, immortal bodies.

- When the saints have disappeared, the world will come under the rule of a dictator called the Antichrist, otherwise known as the "beast", and he will be supported by a second beast called the "false prophet". The reign of Antichrist is known as the "tribulation" and it will last for seven years.

- While there is tribulation on earth, there is a wedding ceremony going on in Heaven, ending with the marriage supper when the saints from the church age will be joined by saints from other ages.

- Jesus, who has already come *for* his saints, will come again *with* his saints, to overthrow the kingdom of the Antichrist and establish his rule on earth for a thousand years. He will overthrow the beast and the false prophet, and will bind the serpent, and the world will be returned to a state of partial but not total perfection. After the thousand years have passed, the serpent will be released for a short while and will deceive the nations, but then he will be defeated altogether.

- There will be a resurrection of unbelievers, for the Final Judgement, and they will be condemned to a fate known as the Second Death.

- The Lord will make a New Heaven and a New Earth as an eternal dwelling place for the believers. There will be a New Jerusalem, and in the city there will be the tree of life, and the saints will live for ever. This new world will be a sinless paradise, as it was in the Garden of Eden.

Chapter 2 - The Pseudo-Gospel

Now that we have looked at the Real Gospel, we will see what happens when certain essential elements are knocked out, leaving us with a Pseudo-Gospel. The word "Gospel" means "good news", and I use the term "Pseudo-Gospel" only for purposes of comparison. In reality, the Pseudo-Gospel is not a Gospel at all, because it does not give any kind of good news, as we shall see.

Why should anyone want to knock out part of the Gospel? What's the point of having a Gospel that is deficient, leaving us with something less than what God has planned for us? The primary motivation is to meet the demands of another competing philosophy called "evolution".

Since the time of Darwin, there has been a growing minority of Christians who believe in evolution, and they have made various efforts to accommodate it within their theology. They developed the so-called "theistic evolution" where each day of creation represents a period of millions of years, and on the occasions where evolution gets into trouble, they say that God intervened and created something, helping evolution along the way. For example, no-one has yet given any reasonable explanation about how the first living cell could have been formed out of ordinary chemicals. At the time of Darwin, understanding of the cell was beginning to increase, but it was still considered to have a relatively simple structure compared with the way we understand it today.[25]

Theistic evolution provides the simple answer, that God came along and issued the creative command, so that the first living cells were formed within the primeval soup. They began to develop into

---

[25] In 1861, only two years after the publication of Darwin's *Origin of Species*, Ernst Wilhelm von Brücke argued that there could be no such thing as a "simple cell" because each cell is an organism that characterises all the complex activity of life. See Perry et. al., *Development of the cell concept*, <www.discoveryofthecell.net>.

multi-celled organisms that eventually became plants, animals and eventually humans. There were many obstacles along the way, but at each point of difficulty, God was always there to help, so that instead of having one big creation, we have a series of mini-creations.

The idea of mini-creations appeared reasonable even to scientists who did not believe in God, so they developed a secular version called "punctuated evolution", where everything remains fairly static for a long time, without much change, and then there is a point where evolution is accelerated, as if it has come into contact with some sort of catalyst, and life jumps forward to a new level.

Theistic evolution has for a long time been of very little interest to Evangelical Christians. It has been primarily the domain of liberal theologians who were regarded with suspicion, apparently capable of perverting the Christian message into any doctrine that suited them. They were never really interested in evangelism, and were more concerned with social issues, so they lived in a theological world that was separate from most Evangelicals. However, they had considerable influence because of their positions within theological colleges. There are many Evangelical church ministers who talk about the time when they were "in the freezer", but they managed to survive it until they got their theological diplomas, then they went somewhere else to get "warmed up".

In recent years, theistic evolution has been making inroads among Evangelicals, so it is no longer just within the domain of liberals. This represents a serious development, because Evangelicals are not content to occupy themselves with social work. Their main activity is preaching and evangelism, and if the Gospel has to be modified to accommodate evolution, what sort of Gospel are they preaching?

Death Before Sin

The biggest problem that arises, by accommodating evolution within the Gospel, is the question of death before sin. If the six days of creation represent millions of years of evolution, it means the process of death and destruction was occurring continuously during that period. The Garden of Eden (if there ever was such a place) would be full of the bones of dead animals, including the ape-like hominids who were the ancestors of Adam and Eve (if these two people actually existed). If Adam was already mortal, what are we to make of the command that he should not eat the forbidden fruit? Let's have a look at the passage again.

> And the Lord God commanded the man, saying, Of every tree of the garden thou mayest freely eat: But of the tree of the knowledge of good and evil, thou shalt not eat of it: for in the day that thou eatest thereof thou shalt surely die.
>
> *Gen. 2:16-17*

If Adam was already expecting to die as soon as the process of ageing and decay had taken its toll, this would be a very confusing statement. Does it mean that the fruit is poisonous, and he would die immediately as soon as he eats it? Evidently not, because this is the tree of the knowledge of good and evil. You don't gain any knowledge by eating poisonous fruit, you just die.

If Adam was already mortal before he took the forbidden fruit, then the consequence of eating it becomes meaningless. If God told him that he would die (eventually) if he took the forbidden fruit, he would have said "So what, I'm going to die anyway. Everybody dies".

Perhaps God could have been a bit more persuasive by telling him that he would be thrown out of the Garden of Eden, and thorns and thistles would grow, and he would have to work by the sweat of his brow, but none of this is mentioned. Perhaps God forgot to tell him.

Later, when the woman is tempted by the serpent, there is the following dialogue:

> Now the serpent was more subtle than any beast of the field which the Lord God had made. And he said unto the woman, Yea, hath God said, Ye shall not eat of every tree of the garden? And the woman said unto the serpent, We may eat of the fruit of the trees of the garden: But of the fruit of the tree which is in the midst of the garden, God hath said, Ye shall not eat of it, neither shall ye touch it, lest ye die. And the serpent said unto the woman, Ye shall not surely die: For God doth

know that in the day ye eat thereof, then your eyes shall be opened, and ye shall be as gods, knowing good and evil.

Gen. 3:1-5

First the serpent questions God's authority, then the woman says that if she eats the fruit (or even touches it, which is her own extension of the command) she will die. If she is already mortal, this statement becomes meaningless.

Then the serpent tells her she will not die, and this is equally meaningless. Either he means that she will not die as a consequence of eating the forbidden fruit because she is going to die anyway, or else he is promising her immortality as a consequence of eating it.

This dialogue, together with all the other dialogues about the forbidden fruit are reduced to absurdities, so that if the "death before sin" doctrine is to be believed, large chunks of text have to be deleted from Genesis 2 and 3. Then when you take into account that the "death before sin" doctrine is just a logical consequence of theistic evolution, which has already tried to reinterpret the story of creation, we can see the consequences of taking on the whole package. The first three chapters of Genesis are left in tatters and might as well be cut out from the Bible altogether.

Sinning that Grace May Abound

If Adam and Eve were not created immortal, the Gospel summarised at the end of Chapter 1 becomes as follows:

- God created the world to include death as part of creation, so that Adam and Eve were both mortals.

- The woman, enticed by the serpent, took the forbidden fruit from the tree of knowledge of good and evil, and ate it. Then she gave it to her husband, and he ate it. They were thrown out of the Garden of Eden, and life became much harder as they had to work for their food, but they did not suffer any eternal consequences because they were mortal already.

- They were given a prophecy, known as the Protevangel, saying that a Messiah, born of a virgin, would come and defeat the serpent, but in the process he would receive an injury.

- After a long history which involved the Flood and the re-population of the world, then the development of the nation of Israel, Jesus the Messiah came. He was fully human, but not under the curse of sin as we are, and he offered himself as the perfect sacrifice, paying the price of our sin, then he rose from the dead, which is really strange because he represents a race of humans who were created mortal and were intended to die. His sacrificial death and resurrection means that all who believe in him can have eternal life, which is really good because we never had eternal life in the first place, at least not in the sense of physical immortality. He appeared to his disciples on a number of occasions, then he ascended into Heaven with the promise that he would return, just as they had seen him go.

- We now live in the church age, when the Gospel is being preached to the world, and those who believe are restored to spiritual life and communion with God. We continue to live in our mortal bodies and will die physically, but we hope that death has no sting, and we hope that our communion with God will continue beyond the grave, although we have some doubts about it because we never had immortality, even before we sinned.

- When Jesus returns, the dead who have believed in him will rise to eternal life. Those who are alive at his coming will also rise and meet him in the air, and we will be forever with the Lord, with transformed, immortal bodies. At least we hope that all this will happen, but for reasons already explained, we can't be sure.

- When the saints have disappeared, the world will come under the rule of a dictator called the Antichrist, otherwise known as the "beast", and he will be supported by a second beast called the "false prophet". The reign of Antichrist is known as the "tribulation" and it will last for seven years.

- While there is tribulation on earth, there is a wedding ceremony going on in Heaven, ending with the marriage supper when the saints from the church age will be joined by saints from other ages.

- Jesus, who has already come *for* his saints, will come again *with* his saints, to overthrow the kingdom of the Antichrist and establish his rule on earth for a thousand years. He will overthrow the beast and the false prophet, and will bind the serpent, and the world will be returned to a state of partial but not total perfection. This is a very nice surprise, considering that the world was very far short of perfection in the first place, with death as part of the natural order. After the thousand years has passed the serpent will be released for a short while and will deceive the nations, but then he will be defeated altogether.

- There will be a resurrection of unbelievers, and they will be condemned to a fate known as the Second Death. Now there's a good one. If humanity was created to die in the first place, does it really matter how many times we die?

- The Lord will make a New Heaven and a New Earth as an eternal dwelling place for the believers. There will be a New Jerusalem, and in the city there will be the tree of life, and the saints will live for ever. This new world will be a sinless paradise, as it was in the Garden of Eden. In that case, the new Garden of Eden is even better than the old one, because in this place we have immortality which we never had before, so it's a good job that we sinned, otherwise we would never enjoy this happy state.

Clearly it's an absurdity to have a Gospel that leaves us better off than we would have been if we had never sinned. The purpose of the Real Gospel is to cancel altogether the effects of the curse and restore us to our former state. The Pseudo-Gospel, if it manages to retain the doctrine of the resurrection of the dead, and all that follows from it, makes us feel good that we got involved in this thing called sin, because we started off mortal, and ended up immortal, so we have cut a very good deal out of it.

Tidying Up the Bible

If we believe that we were created mortal, and we want a consistent theology that doesn't make us better off by sinning, we have to make sure that we end up mortal. Perhaps we would like to imagine that we could achieve immortality by some power of our own, that has nothing to do with sin and salvation, but this has already been denied to us because we were forbidden access to the tree of life. In that case, we have to be satisfied with our mortality and a few more chunks of the Bible have to be cut out.

> And the angel answered and said unto the women, Fear not ye: for I know that ye seek Jesus, which was crucified. He is not here: for he is risen, as he said. Come, see the place where the Lord lay. And go quickly, and tell his disciples that he is risen from the dead; and, behold, he goeth before you into Galilee; there shall ye see him: lo, I have told you.
>
> *Matt. 28:5-7*

The passage about the resurrection of Jesus would have to go because it would serve no purpose if mortality was part of the created order. Just think about it for a moment. God creates the world and populates it with men and women who die, but before they die, they reproduce, and another generation appears. The cycle of life and death continues, and it goes on indefinitely as long as the gene pool can be maintained without too many destructive mutations. If this is what God intended, it could even be described as "good", as in Genesis 1 where several times we have the phrase "God saw that it was good". If the propagation of our genes in successive generations is the primary objective of our creation, then the death of an individual should not be considered a problem. In that case, the resurrection of Jesus would serve no purpose and would actually be a violation of the created order. Instead of rising from the dead, he should have got married and produced offspring the same as the rest of us.

There is nothing new about the arguments being presented here. Every branch of Greek philosophy considers death to be normal, and this is why the Greeks mocked Paul when he spoke of the resurrection of the dead.

And they that conducted Paul brought him unto Athens: ... Then certain philosophers of the Epicureans, and of the Stoicks, encountered him. And some said, What will this babbler say? other some, He seemeth to be a setter forth of strange gods: because he preached unto them Jesus, and the resurrection. ... Then Paul stood in the midst of Mars' hill, and said, Ye men of Athens, I perceive that in all things ye are too superstitious. For as I passed by, and beheld your devotions, I found an altar with this inscription, TO THE UNKNOWN GOD. Whom therefore ye ignorantly worship, him declare I unto you. God that made the world and all things therein, seeing that he is Lord of heaven and earth, dwelleth not in temples made with hands; Neither is worshipped with men's hands, as though he needed any thing, seeing he giveth to all life, and breath, and all things; ... For in him we live, and move, and have our being; ... And the times of this ignorance God winked at; but now commandeth all men every where to repent: Because he hath appointed a day, in the which he will judge the world in righteousness by that man whom he hath ordained; whereof he hath given assurance unto all men, in that he hath raised him from the dead. And when they heard of the resurrection of the dead, some mocked: and others said, We will hear thee again of this matter. So Paul departed from among them.

Acts 17:15-33

There are basically three branches of Greek Philosophy, with regard to life and death:

- The Epicureans believed that our entire existence depends on the physical senses, so that both body and soul disintegrate at death.

- The Stoics believed that the body returns to the earth, but the soul is a spark from the original fire and it continues for a while after death, but eventually returns to the fire from which it came.

- The Platonists,[26] not mentioned here, but very influential, believed that we have an immortal soul which departs from the body at death and goes to an unseen, invisible world, and then returns and inhabits another body. So they believed in reincarnation.

---

[26] Jowett, Benjamin, *Plato's Dialogues: Phaedo*, <www.bartleby.com/2/1/31.html>.

None of them believed in the resurrection of the dead, in the way that Paul was preaching. After Paul had put up with some mockery from the Epicureans and the Stoics, he went to Mars Hill and preached a creation message, saying *"God that made the world and all things therein, ..."* He knew that their problems with the resurrection were derived from their lack of understanding of creation. If he could convince them that *"in him we live, and move, and have our being"*, then perhaps they would see that death is a consequence of sin, and he called them to repentance. But when he spoke of the resurrection of the dead, they started mocking again. Their beliefs about life and death were too entrenched, and they were not going to give them up just because an itinerant preacher had arrived.

If we are also entrenched in the belief that death is normal, then this passage is lost as far as Christianity is concerned, because it means that Paul was wrong and the Greek philosophers were right.

Even among the church there were people who thought there was no resurrection of the dead. Obviously they were under the influence of Greek philosophy, and Paul addressed the problem as follows:

> Now if Christ be preached that he rose from the dead, how say some among you that there is no resurrection of the dead? But if there be no resurrection of the dead, then is Christ not risen: And if Christ be not risen, then is our preaching vain, and your faith is also vain. Yea, and we are found false witnesses of God; because we have testified of God that he raised up Christ: whom he raised not up, if so be that the dead rise not. For if the dead rise not, then is not Christ raised: And if Christ be not raised, your faith is vain; ye are yet in your sins. Then they also which are fallen asleep in Christ are perished. If in this life only we have hope in Christ, we are of all men most miserable. But now is Christ risen from the dead, and become the firstfruits of them that slept. For since by man came death, by man came also the resurrection of the dead. For as in Adam all die, even so in Christ shall all be made alive. But every man in his own order: Christ the firstfruits; afterward they that are Christ's at his coming.

1 Cor. 15:12-23

Notice the logic of this. Paul is not using the resurrection of Christ to prove that there is a resurrection of all believers. He is doing it the other way round. He is saying that if there is no resurrection of believers, then Christ is not raised. Christ is considered the first of many to be raised from the dead, and the same theme appears in another of Paul's letters.

> And he is the head of the body, the church: who is the beginning, the firstborn from the dead; that in all things he might have the preeminence.
>
> *Col. 1:18*

Returning to the passage from Corinthians, we find something that would cause deep embarrassment to the church if there was no resurrection of the dead. When Paul refers to those who are *"fallen asleep in Christ"* he means the martyrs, and they would all have died in vain if salvation was only for this life. What would he say to the church, and especially to the families of those who had given their lives as martyrs, if he changed his mind and decided that there was no resurrection? Would he say "Sorry, I was mistaken" and face up to their wrath, or would he pretend that he believed it and watch more people getting martyred? Paul and his companions would certainly have been *"of all men most miserable"* if they thought that there was no resurrection. But they were never in that dilemma, because they knew that Christ had been raised, and he gave the evidence for it:

> For I delivered unto you first of all that which I also received, how that Christ died for our sins according to the scriptures; And that he was buried, and that he rose again the third day according to the scriptures: And that he was seen of Cephas, then of the twelve: After that, he was seen of above five hundred brethren at once; of whom the greater part remain unto this present, but some are fallen asleep. After that, he was seen of James; then of all the apostles. And last of all he was seen of me also, as of one born out of due time.
>
> *1 Cor. 15:3-8*

The cycle of life and death, over a long period of time, provides the basis of evolution, which is a scientifically packaged version of

Greek philosophy. The Greeks believed that life came from the sea, and we will deal with this question in Appendix 1.

Evolution and Greek philosophy both share the view that death is normal. The Greek philosophers took the obvious next step, and rejected Paul's teaching about the resurrection, and modern-day evolutionist Christians will also have to make up their minds about this question. You can't have it both ways. Either you have evolution, with its doctrine of death before sin, or else you have the resurrection. If you choose evolution, all the above passages will have to be deleted from the Bible, and all the passages in Chapter 1 that refer to the resurrection.

Chapters 21 and 22 of Revelation would also have to be deleted, almost in their entirety, because they are about the New Heaven and the New Earth, and the description of the New Jerusalem and the Tree of Life. The deletion of text from the Book of Revelation causes especially serious problems, because there is a specific curse on anyone who does it.

> For I testify unto every man that heareth the words of the prophecy of this book, If any man shall add unto these things, God shall add unto him the plagues that are written in this book: And if any man shall take away from the words of the book of this prophecy, God shall take away his part out of the book of life, and out of the holy city, and from the things which are written in this book.
>
> *Rev. 22:18-19*

There are many more passages that would have to be deleted, and if I were to list them all, the Bible would be so badly messed up, it would not be worth reading.

The Pseudo-Gospel in Practice

Churches that preach the Pseudo-Gospel don't normally put up a big sign saying "We believe in evolution" or "We were created mortal and there is no resurrection". Instead it's much more subtle. They preach something that sounds like an Evangelical message, but they emphasise this world rather than the next. They preach about how Jesus can set you free from your messed up life, and sometimes they use Biblical terms such as sin, salvation, and eternal life, but it all means something slightly different.

Sin means messing up your life, as if you have sinned against yourself, rather than against God. Salvation means getting your life sorted out. Eternal life, if it is mentioned at all, means that we enjoy the presence of God in this life, and it continues beyond the grave in a spiritual dimension called heaven, but nobody seems to know whether it's our final destination or a temporary resting place while we wait for something else. They don't understand it much and prefer to concern themselves with this life rather than the next.

If salvation means fixing up your messed up life, it becomes irrelevant for people who haven't got one. When I became a Christian, I was living at home with my Mum and Dad and my two brothers, and we all had lots of nice friends, and I was getting on with my schoolwork. I wasn't perfect by any means (at least that's what my Mum tells me) but I wasn't into crime and drugs, or any of the things that would define a messed up life by today's standards. If someone had said to me "Jesus can sort out your messed up life", I wouldn't have been interested. I became a Christian because I was told that Jesus died on the cross and rose again to secure my ***eternal*** salvation, not just something perishable that would last only for this life.

In its extreme version, the Pseudo-Gospel teaches that all the problems of this life can be fixed instantly. There is a strong emphasis on healing and deliverance, and if someone is having problems with their marriage, the demons that are messing it up are bound in the name of Jesus and the problem is fixed, or so they think. If you have financial problems, you "name it and claim it", or you "smite your debt" (and this includes people who are in debt because they have indulged in excessive luxuries and can't afford to pay for them). Very few people get saved through this type of evangelism, and if they think they are saved, they don't know what it means. If salvation is for this world only, it means they might expect to get some positive results from their next healing and deliverance meeting, but that's as far as it goes.

For the preachers of the Pseudo-Gospel, the question of creation and evolution is not much of an issue. The resurrection to eternal life is not very high on their agenda, and therefore they don't need to concern themselves with the state of humanity before the fall, or perhaps they have never made the connection between the two. They assume, wrongly, that evolution has won all the scientific arguments, and they don't want to offend the middle-class professionals in their congregation by suggesting otherwise.

Coming Out of the Pseudo-Gospel

There are two ways out of the Pseudo-Gospel, depending on what you do with evolution.

• Abandon evolution and believe the Real Gospel.

• Stick with evolution and abandon Christianity.

At this point I hear some people protesting. "We can't abandon evolution, it's a proven scientific fact, so what choice have we got?" The answer is that you do have a choice. Evolution is not a proven fact, it's a philosophical viewpoint that attempts to reconstruct the past on the basis of present-day observations. There is more than one way to reconstruct the past from the same data, and we will look into this in Appendix 1.

In any case, there have never been any proven facts that run contrary to God's Word. There have been many occasions where God has asked people to believe something, contrary to some supposed evidence, and there are many heroes of faith who have believed God's Word when apparently all the evidence was against them. There is a list of these heroes in Hebrews 11, including Abel, Enoch, Noah, Abraham, Sarah, Isaac, Jacob, Joseph, Moses, Rahab, Gideon, Barak, Samson, Jephthah, David, Samuel and a host of un-named prophets.

However, you don't need to be a hero of faith to reject evolution today. There is so much evidence to the contrary, that it takes more faith to be an evolutionist than a creationist, but we will deal with that in the Appendices.

To come out of the Pseudo-Gospel, and believe the Real Gospel, you simply have to decide that you believe what the Bible says, including the account of creation, the fall, the flood, the crucifixion and resurrection of Jesus, the resurrection of believers, and the resurrection of unbelievers at the Final Judgement.

This does not mean committing intellectual suicide. The arguments of science might rage around our heads, sometimes in favour of evolution, and sometimes in favour of creation, but the Word of God is our sure foundation. God is patient, and waits for those who doubt. Some of the heroes of faith showed their weaknesses, for example Thomas who would not believe in the resurrection of Jesus until he had seen and touched the wounds in his hands and side. Jesus never rebuked him for his lack of faith. Instead he appeared to him and gave him the evidence he needed.

Throwing Away the Baggage

Let's face it, most people don't have time to go into all the arguments about creation and evolution. It would be a full-time job, keeping up to speed with all the latest developments on both sides. We have to go to work, to earn money, and if we are involved in a church, we might be involved in the youth group, or some other essential activity. Most of us would accept that the youth work is essential because without it there is no future for the church. We can't all drop everything and become full-time specialists in Creation Science, but we do need specialists who can reduce the data to manageable quantities and give us a reasonable interpretation of the facts, and present it in such a way that we can check it out for ourselves.

Throughout our lives we believe things that other people tell us, because we respect their integrity, and sometimes we find that our judgement has been misguided, so we go in search of someone else who can give us better advice. We end up with a collection of baggage that we never have time to prove or disprove, and we just try to muddle along with it.

The continual presentation of evolution as a supposedly proven fact is probably the worst collection of baggage that anyone can be expected to endure. It screams out at us from everywhere, in the school books and on TV, without any proof, and without even the slightest suggestion that alternative interpretations might be possible. You turn on the TV and watch a natural history programme and it tells us what happened "millions of years ago", but nobody was there at the time to see what actually happened. The presenter shows us a fossil and says "this is the ultimate proof of evolution" but he doesn't say why it constitutes proof. The Piltdown Man was considered to be proof of evolution for forty years, until someone took the trouble to look at it carefully and discovered that it was a deliberate fake. The embarrassment of this affair has healed through the passage of time, and the media continues to scream out "evolution", and they know that if they repeat it often enough, people will believe it.

Not only is it repetitive, it's also oppressive. Evolutionists have gained control of research institutions so that creationists among their staff can be dismissed if they are discovered. When creationists want to do research, using facilities that they have paid for out of their own taxpayer's money, they have to get on with their work quietly, pretending to be evolutionists, or at least trying to avoid the subject. When they get a result that supports creation, they can't discuss it openly with their colleagues, and instead they have to pass it on secretly to creationist organisations. It's rather like the old days of the Soviet Union where "secret believers" would work for the KGB and would tip off the underground church when they thought it was in danger.

There is obviously a difference between a serious, committed evolutionist and someone who simply gets on with their life, carrying around the baggage imposed on them by the evolutionist media. Most evolutionists are just carrying baggage, and when they become Christians, they continue to carry the baggage for a while, and need to throw it off. They used to be evolutionist non-Christians, and now they are evolutionist Christians, but it's their Christian belief that really matters, and the evolutionist baggage is irrelevant by comparison. They need to throw off the baggage, because in time it will catch up with them, as they begin to have problems with some of the issues I have already mentioned.

The early Christians also used to carry baggage. They lived in a culture of paganism, and when a pagan became a Christian, he would have to work through all his pagan philosophies, one by one, and re-learn everything from a Christian point of view. The Christians at Corinth, who questioned the resurrection of the dead, were probably just carrying around baggage, and Paul was helping them to throw it off.

There is a certain amount of baggage that has to be thrown off before someone can become a Christian, and there might be occasions where someone thinks they have become a Christian but they actually haven't. For example, if someone has been taught the Pseudo-Gospel and has responded to a message that is just for this life, and has nothing to do with eternity, they will have to be converted all over again when they hear the Real Gospel.

There is an example of a second conversion in the Book of Acts, where some people had believed the teaching of John the Baptist, but never fully understood what it means to believe in Jesus and receive salvation. The message of John the Baptist was not any kind of Pseudo Gospel. It was the Real Gospel in his time, but he never saw much of the ministry of Jesus because he was beheaded. His message was to prepare the way of the Lord, by preaching a baptism of repentance. The relevant passage is as follows:

> And it came to pass, that, while Apollos was at Corinth, Paul having passed through the upper coasts came to Ephesus: and finding certain disciples, He said unto them, Have ye received the Holy Ghost since ye believed? And they said unto him, We have not so much as heard whether there be any Holy Ghost. And he said unto them, Unto what then were ye baptized? And they said, Unto John's baptism. Then said Paul, John verily baptized with the baptism of repentance, saying unto the people, that they should believe on him which should come after him, that is, on Christ Jesus. When they heard this, they were baptized in the name of the Lord Jesus. And when Paul had laid his hands upon them, the Holy Ghost came on them; and they spake with tongues, and prophesied. And all the men were about twelve.
>
> *Acts 19:1-7*

This passage has been used by Pentecostal Christians to argue in favour of a "second blessing" where you receive the Holy Spirit in a special way, some time after conversion, and you are equipped with spiritual gifts such as speaking in tongues, prophecy, healing, etc. I believe that the true position on this is that we receive the Holy Spirit, and have full access to these gifts, from the time of our conversion. In that case, I disagree with the Pentecostals, but I also disagree with the Evangelicals who deny the "second blessing" because for the most part they deny the use of spiritual gifts altogether, saying that they were only available to the early church and are not for our time.

Anyway, putting aside the Pentecostal/Evangelical debate, what exactly is this passage about? Paul has come across some people who appear to be believers, and he says *"Have you received the Holy Ghost since you believed?"* The word "since" does not mean "after". Instead it indicates consequence, for example we might say "Since I am forgetful, I will write a note." Paul means "Have you received the Holy Spirit as a consequence of believing?" There is actually no Greek word in this passage that means "since" and it literally means "Believing, did you receive the Holy Spirit?"

From their response to the question, Paul discovers that they never understood the true Gospel of salvation, and he explains it to them properly, and they are saved.

The same situation applies to people who have believed the Pseudo-Gospel. If they have trusted in Jesus to sort out their messed up lives, and nothing more, their supposed salvation is ineffective. They need to hear the Real Gospel and get saved properly.

My advice to any new Christian is as follows:

- Throw off all the baggage of evolution. Just forget it, and in the process of time, try to go through all the creation/evolution arguments again from scratch. Of course there will be many other things to learn, so don't try to do it all at once. Get some creationist books and magazines and compare them with the evolutionist theories that you used to believe. See Appendices 5 and 6 for some useful organisations and resources.

- Read your Bible, and especially pay attention to all the passages about the resurrection. Have you been taught anything that looks like the Pseudo-Gospel? If so, complain to your church leaders about it. If they are indifferent to the issue, don't waste time with them. Just find someone else who believes the Real Gospel. If it turns out that you have responded to the Pseudo-Gospel, without understanding what Jesus really offers, it means you are not really saved, and you need to get saved properly.

Chapter 3 - Keeping the Faith

> And he spake many things unto them in parables, saying, Behold, a sower went forth to sow; And when he sowed, some seeds fell by the way side, and the fowls came and devoured them up: Some fell upon stony places, where they had not much earth: and forthwith they sprung up, because they had no deepness of earth: And when the sun was up, they were scorched; and because they had no root, they withered away. And some fell among thorns; and the thorns sprung up, and choked them: But other fell into good ground, and brought forth fruit, some an hundredfold, some sixtyfold, some thirtyfold.
>
> *Matt. 13:3-8*

Jesus explained to his disciples that in this parable, the seed represents the Word of God, and the ground on which it falls represents four types of circumstances in which a person might receive it:

- The path is a place where there is no fertile soil, and when the person hears the Word, he doesn't understand it. The Devil immediately snatches it away, like the birds of the air.

- The stony ground is a place where there is a small amount of fertile soil, but mostly stones, and this represents the person who hears the Word and receives it, but cannot put down roots, and gives up when there is persecution.

- The thorns represent the cares of this world and the pursuit of wealth, so that when the seed falls on this type of ground it becomes choked. The person has heard the Word but has become distracted with other things.

- The good ground represents the person who hears the Word and understands it, and "bears fruit", meaning he studies it to learn more, and he teaches it to others, so that it multiplies.

This simple parable is taught to every child at Sunday School, even in churches that teach the Pseudo-Gospel. It is usually assumed that most of the people who appear regularly in church are in the fourth category, where the seed falls on good ground and bears fruit, but in many churches this is not the case, as we shall see when we look at the activity-based church on page 97.

Jesus taught two other parables that represent the theme of growth:

- The mustard seed that grew into a great tree.

- The yeast that makes the dough rise.

Then he moved on to a different type of parable, where the seed does not represent the Word of God. Instead it represents the people who believe it.

> Another parable put he forth unto them, saying, The kingdom of heaven is likened unto a man which sowed good seed in his field: But while men slept, his enemy came and sowed tares among the wheat, and went his way. But when the blade was sprung up, and brought forth fruit, then appeared the tares also. So the servants of the householder came and said unto him, Sir, didst not thou sow good seed in thy field? from whence then hath it tares? He said unto them, An enemy hath done this. The servants said unto him, Wilt thou then that we go and gather them up? But he said, Nay; lest while ye gather up the tares, ye root up also the wheat with them. Let both grow together until the harvest: and in the time of harvest I will say to the reapers, Gather ye together first the tares, and bind them in bundles to burn them: but gather the wheat into my barn.
>
> *Matt. 13: 24-30*

This is part of a collection of parables where Jesus identifies something of value, sometimes comparing it with something worthless.

His disciples asked him about the meaning of the parable, and he explained that the good seed, which grows into wheat, represents the "children of the kingdom", and the weeds are the "children of the wicked one". The wheat and weeds are allowed to grow together, and then they are separated during the harvest at the end of the world.

The other parables in this collection are:

- The man who finds treasure in a field, so he puts it back where he found it and buys the field so that he can legally possess the treasure.

- The merchant who found a pearl of great price, so he sold all that he had and bought it.

- The fishermen who drew up all kinds of fish in their net, and when they went ashore they put the good fish into baskets and threw the bad fish away.

When Jesus had finished talking about his parables, he asked the disciples whether they had understood them, and they said *"Yes, Lord"*, then he said:

> Therefore every scribe which is instructed unto the kingdom of heaven is like unto a man that is an householder, which bringeth forth out of his treasure things new and old.
>
> *Matt. 13:52*

Now he is talking about the fourth category in his first parable, where the seed, representing the Word of God, falls on good ground. One of the characteristics of a true believer is that he is always studying the Bible and teaching it to others, according to his capacity. Out of his treasure he brings out the "old" things, meaning the established doctrine of his church that might have remained the same for centuries, and the "new" things that he has just discovered. Some of the new things might have been there all the time and been forgotten, for example interpretations of the Bible that depend on an understanding of Jewish history and culture, and have been neglected because of the long separation of Christians and Jews. Also, among the new things there might be interpretations of prophecy that relate to modern events, or scientific discoveries that support the Bible (yes, there are many of them).

A true believer should always be able to make the Bible interesting, or at least be able to sit down with a good teacher and enjoy listening to whatever he can bring out of his store of treasure.

However, we have to make sure it really is treasure and not falsehood. When we bring out "new" things, they have to be newly discovered truths, not new doctrines that we have invented to conform to the modern world. We don't follow the world, we follow Jesus, and we get our doctrine from the Bible, by reading it according to the history and context in which it was written.

Big-Name Ministries

All believers are called to communicate their faith to others in some way, even if it just means talking to our friends and colleagues at work when the opportunity arises. Some of us are called into full-time ministry, and for a few of us, it means a high-profile ministry that reaches thousands of people, or perhaps even millions.

The bigger the ministry, the more is expected, and the person at the centre of it all has to know the answers to everything. It's important, therefore, not to over-stretch ourselves, and we should only undertake ministries for which we are fully equipped, and the more we seek to reach out to others, the more we have to study.

Unfortunately, society has a habit of throwing up superstars, giving them status and influence that is quite disproportionate to their actual ability. For example, a stand-up comedian who is used to performing in pubs and clubs might be spotted by someone and offered a TV contract that enables him to perform in front of millions. He has been selected because he is considered to be good, but he might not be all that much better than his contemporaries who are still doing the pubs and clubs. Certainly, he is not thousands of times better, but his responsibility might be thousands of times greater if he comes out with a bad joke that people consider to be offensive.

Superstars are selected on the basis of their style and presentation, and whether or not they look good for the role. Unfortunately, the same thing sometimes happens in the church. Big-name speakers are propelled to stardom on the basis of their style and presentation, but when you consider the content of what they have said, it could have been done by almost anyone who warms a pew on Sundays. Then if you want to talk to them and ask a question, you find that they hide behind an organisation and don't really have time for personal dialogue. You end up having to talk to the minister or elders of your own church, asking them "What was it that the visiting preacher said?"

When someone's ministry reaches the scale of mass evangelism, for example Billy Graham, the organisation becomes almost entirely a substitute for personal dialogue. You can't ask Billy Graham a question. You have to ask his organisation, and a secretary will try and answer it from his books or magazine articles, or an archive of questions that have been asked already. Only in a small minority of cases is the question passed to Billy Graham himself.

However, it doesn't matter how elaborate the organisation is, the big-name speaker is still at the top, and it remains a fair generalisation that the bigger your ministry, the more you have to study. This became starkly obvious when Charles Templeton, a contemporary of Billy Graham with similar communication skills, went into big-time ministry on the same scale as Billy Graham, but without any preparation and he had not even finished his high school education. He eventually went to Princeton Theological Seminary which is notorious for its liberal teaching, and then he continued his big-time ministry for a few more years, but it became too much for him and he gave it up. He didn't just give up the ministry. He publicly renounced his faith and became an agnostic. After leading thousands to Christ, he could not sustain his own faith because he had long-standing doubts that were never resolved. The problem was, he never participated in study and informal group dialogue during the early days, and never experienced the growth phase that is normal for most new Christians.

Whatever our ministry might be, we have to get down to some serious study, to find out what we really believe, and how to communicate it to others. All believers are called to be evangelists, even if it's just in a small, relatively insignificant way. Everyone who passes through the church gate is a witness to the community outside, even if we only go there to clean the floor, and we have to be ready to give an answer to anyone who asks us about our faith.

Generally, the bigger our ministry, the more we become responsible for answering questions, and the more we have to study.

The church cleaner can easily say "You need to talk to the minister", but then what is the minister supposed to do, if he doesn't know the answers? He doesn't have the same opportunities to pass things upwards. In some cases, he might be able to use the resources of a specialist organisation. For example if it's a question about creation and evolution, he might be able to refer them to one of the creationist organisations listed in Appendix 5, but at the end of the day, he has to know something about the subject.

The Apostle Paul (originally called Saul) considered study to be a matter of primary importance for anyone involved in ministry, and wrote to Timothy as follows:

> Study to show thyself approved unto God, a workman that needeth not to be ashamed, rightly dividing the word of truth.
>
> *2 Tim. 2:15*

He was especially diligent in preparation for his own ministry, although he had plenty of time for it because he had previously persecuted the church, and for a while the believers wouldn't trust him. The events of his conversion and preparation for ministry can be found by stitching together various passages from Acts and Galatians:

- He was on his way to Damascus to persecute the church, but was converted to Christ while on the journey, and he was also struck blind. (Acts 9:1-9).

- A believer called Ananias, who lived in Damascus, received Paul, in spite of his reputation for persecuting the church, and he did so because he had been given special instructions from God. He also laid hands on Paul and his sight was restored, and then Paul was baptised and remained a few days with the believers in Damascus. (Acts 9:10-19).

- Paul preached in the synagogues at Damascus, but the Jews plotted to kill him, and he escaped by being let down by the wall in a basket. (Acts 9:20-25).

- He went to Arabia (which bordered on Syria at that time), then returned to Damascus. (Gal. 1:17).

- After three years he went to Jerusalem, but the churches were afraid of him because of his reputation and didn't accept him as a believer. However, Barnabas took him to see the apostles, including Peter and James[27]. (Acts 9:26-27; Gal. 1:18).

- He began preaching to the Greeks, but they tried to kill him, and when the believers heard about it, they sent him back to his home town of Tarsus in Cilicia. He travelled there through Caesarea and Syria. (Acts 9:28-30; Gal. 1:21).

- The churches grew in Judea, Galilee and Samaria, free from persecution, and they gradually began to accept that Paul, now in a state of exile, had become a genuine believer. (Acts 9:31; Gal. 1:22-24).

- Eventually, Barnabas went to Tarsus to get Paul and brought him to Antioch and they stayed there for a year, teaching the church. (Acts 11:25-26).

- There was a prophecy about a famine, and Paul, Barnabas and Titus were sent to Jerusalem on a relief visit. By this time, fourteen years had passed since Paul's conversion, and the believers had overcome their fear of him and were ready to accept him. Paul believed that God had called him to a ministry among the Gentiles, and the apostles gave him the *"right hands of fellowship"* so that he could start his ministry. (Acts 11:27-30; Gal. 2:1-10).

- Paul and Barnabas returned to Antioch, with John Mark. There were prophets in the church who prayed and fasted, and the Holy Spirit said *"Separate me Barnabas and Saul[28] for the work whereunto I have called them"*, and they were sent out on their first evangelistic journey. (Acts 12:25 - 13:3).

---

[27] There are a number of people in the New Testament called James. This one is the brother of Jesus.

[28] Paul was still using his old name Saul at this point. His name was changed to Paul soon after the beginning of his first evangelistic journey (Acts 13:9).

Paul's preparation for ministry must have been primarily the long period of time that he spent in Tarsus, before Barnabas came to get him and brought him to Antioch. When they arrived in Antioch, Paul began actively ministering to the local church and received the official approval of the apostles in Jerusalem a year later, as a mature believer of fourteen years standing. He believed that God had specifically called him to preach to the Gentiles, and he describes his experience in Jerusalem like this:

> Then fourteen years after[29] I went up again to Jerusalem with Barnabas, and took Titus with me also. And I went up by revelation, and communicated unto them that gospel which I preach among the Gentiles, but privately to them which were of reputation, lest by any means I should run, or had run, in vain. But neither Titus, who was with me, being a Greek, was compelled to be circumcised: And that because of false brethren unawares brought in, who came in privily to spy out our liberty which we have in Christ Jesus, that they might bring us into bondage: To whom we gave place by subjection, no, not for an hour; that the truth of the gospel might continue with you. But of these who seemed to be somewhat, (whatsoever they were, it maketh no matter to me: God accepteth no man's person:) for they who seemed to be somewhat in conference added nothing to me: But contrariwise, when they saw that the gospel of the uncircumcision was committed unto me, as the gospel of the circumcision was unto Peter; (For he that wrought effectually in Peter to the apostleship of the circumcision, the same was mighty in me toward the Gentiles:) And when James, Cephas, and John, who seemed to be pillars, perceived the grace that was given unto me, they gave to me and Barnabas the right hands of fellowship; that we should go unto the heathen, and they unto the circumcision.
>
> *Gal. 2:1-9*

---

[29] This should be taken to mean fourteen years after Paul's conversion, bringing the date to about AD 46. See Davidson, *The New Bible Commentary*.

At that time, the Gospel had only been preached to Jewish people, and to so-called "God-fearers"[30] who had an affiliation with Judaism. Paul was about to embark on a mission, preaching to Gentiles who had no connection with Judaism, and he would not expect them to convert to Judaism or become circumcised. He knew it would be a controversial message, and before preaching it to the world, he wanted to preach it privately *"to them which are of reputation"*, meaning the Apostles themselves. It must have been rather like the practice sessions that are held at some Bible colleges, where a student is asked to preach a sermon to his tutor and fellow-students, so they can criticise his doctrine and style of delivery before letting him loose on a congregation.

Paul had done some preaching when he first became a believer, and during his first visit to Jerusalem. Then he spent a long time in Tarsus, most probably engaged in private study and some relatively low-profile ministry. Then he spent a year in Antioch with Barnabas, ministering to the church and was eventually considered to be ready for his first evangelistic journey. His long period of preparation meant that he was certain of his calling, and would not run in vain preaching a doctrine that eventually turns out to be false.

He encouraged the believers at Corinth to run the same race as himself, but even after all his years of preparation, he considered the possibility that his ministry could fail if he allowed his message to become corrupted:

> Know ye not that they which run in a race run all, but one receiveth the prize? So run, that ye may obtain. And every man that striveth for the mastery is temperate in all things. Now they do it to obtain a corruptible crown; but we an incorruptible. I therefore so run, not as uncertainly; so fight I, not as one that beateth the air: But I keep under my body, and bring it into subjection: lest that by any means, when I have preached to others, I myself should be a castaway.
>
> *1 Cor. 9:24-27*

---

[30] A "God-fearer" is a Gentile who attends the synagogue and observes some of the Jewish customs but does not fully convert to Judaism and does not become circumcised. An example is Cornelius who is described as *"one that feared God"*. (Acts 10:2)

The reference to his "body" is just figurative language derived from Greek athletic contests. He isn't doing anything physical. He is simply maintaining the quality of his doctrine so that he can preach a clear message wherever he goes, and not allow it to be undermined by local philosophies. The Greek *adokimos*, translated "castaway" means "not approved", or "counterfeit". It doesn't imply that he could lose his salvation. Instead, it means that his doctrine could be corrupted so that it becomes useless for evangelism. Paul knew what he believed, but he always had to present it in a way that was meaningful to other cultures. For example, when he went to Athens he found an altar to the "Unknown God"[31] and used it as the basis for his sermon. (Acts 17:23). It worked well enough, and a few people believed, but for the most part the Greeks rejected his message when he spoke of the resurrection of the dead. Some of them wanted to discuss the matter further, but Paul went away, obviously convinced that prolonged debate with the Greek philosophers would get nowhere. Perhaps he might have been concerned that they would accept his message on their own terms, and they would make up their own Hellenised version of the faith, and then he would have another heresy to contend with. He had given them the true gospel, and that was all he was prepared to give.

Other, less educated men, might have looked for elements of the Greek philosophy that can be matched up with Christianity, on the basis that many pagan beliefs are simply a corruption of the true faith that was taught by the ancient patriarchs. They might have gone further, starting with the altar to the Unknown God, and moving on to other aspects of pagan belief, but Paul knew that if he went along this road with the Greeks he would end up with an ecumenical interfaith hybrid that would be no use to anyone. He didn't want to go to his next place of ministry and hear people saying "What is Paul preaching?"

---

[31] This might be a reference to the One True God who the Greeks had forgotten. There is evidence of early monotheism in many pagan religions. See Hales, R.L., *The Original World Monotheism*, <www.creationism.org/csshs/v07n2p18.htm>.

Finding the Real Gospel

About three decades ago, it was possible to go almost anywhere in the UK and find a church that preaches the Real Gospel. There were also some churches that preached the Pseudo-Gospel, or some variation of it, and they were commonly known as liberals. You could easily distinguish between the different types of church, because those that preached the Real Gospel did so with passion and conviction, and if you asked them a question about something they would come straight out with the answer. The liberals didn't have such a great emphasis on preaching. They would preach a sermon at each of their church services, but it wasn't the most important part of the service, and it generally lacked substance. People didn't go there for the sermon, they went there for the songs, the liturgies and the traditions. They were more interested in social action than spiritual ministry, but in practice their social action probably never exceeded the people who preached the Real Gospel. I could find plenty of people who preached the Real Gospel and they found time to help those who were sick, or bereaved, or in trouble in some way, and they generously supported charitable causes. The difference between the preachers of the Real Gospel and the Pseudo Gospel was not in their lifestyles and social actions, but in their beliefs and how they communicated them. The preachers of the Real Gospel could easily give you a scenario similar to what I have described in Chapter 1, although there were minor differences of doctrine. The liberals, if they took any interest in theology at all, would give you such a wide range of different views, you didn't know where you were. It was actually difficult to associate a theology with a church, because their collective view consisted of the sum of all the views of their members, including those who didn't seem to have any views about anything.

The Real Gospel was preached in churches that would call themselves Evangelical, and although this term could be applied to any church that sought to make converts, it usually meant Protestant Evangelical churches such as Baptists, Pentecostals and a wide range of other denominations including some Anglicans. The easiest way to find the Real Gospel being preached was to go to any church that is considered to be in the Evangelical camp, and listen to just one of their sermons. Normally the content and style of delivery would be enough to tell you what they believed, but if you were still not sure, you could ask the pastor or one of the elders, or almost anyone else in the congregation. Normally it would be enough to wait until they had finished the last hymn and the benediction, and then you could turn to the person next to you and say "Hello, I'm new here, can you tell me about this church?" and they would tell you everything.

Once you had found a good church, you could spend as much time as you liked discussing what they believed, and it was encouraged. In addition to the Sunday services, they would have mid-week meetings, either in the church building or in somebody's house, and they would read a passage of the Bible and discuss it. If there was anything you didn't understand, you could say "What does this mean?" In some churches, a few people would get together, without any supervision from the leadership, and hold Bible study meetings in their homes, and the leaders didn't mind, as long as it contributed to the life of the church and didn't become a splinter group. This type of activity was possible because Christians were generally well educated in spiritual and theological matters. They knew how to use commentaries, concordances and Bible dictionaries, and they knew a bit of church history, and some of them knew a bit of Hebrew and Greek. Occasionally, you would find someone with no formal theological training, and no official position in the church, and he was just a pew-warmer on Sundays, but at the mid-week meeting it became obvious that he knew more than everybody else including the pastor and all the elders. Some pastors used to fear this type of person, because the pastor was supposed to be ahead of everybody else, but there was nothing he could do except to welcome the advanced student as one of the hazards of the job.

Activity-Based Church

Now we come to the present time, and things don't seem to be the same any more. It's not so easy to find the Real Gospel, and there doesn't seem to be so many people studying the Bible. Instead of Bible study, we have a multitude of other activities, all geared towards presentation rather than content. In the old days we used to open the Bible and read it, and that was all we needed, but now it has to be a multi-media presentation, or if it's a small group you can do a game or a role-play that has a very simple message.

To a great extent it's because people have become accustomed to high-quality visual presentations, especially on TV where large amounts of money are available for programme preparation. The education system has also changed so that lessons are much more interactive. When I went to school we had a mixture of lectures and practical sessions. Sometimes we would listen to the teacher for 40 minutes and make notes, and sometimes, especially in the science classes, we would do experiments. Given the choice, most of us would have preferred to do something practical, but if we had to listen to a lecture we could do it. We were just normal kids, not perfect by any means, but we accepted that the lesson type depended on what was being taught, and sometimes it meant listening to a lecture. Nowadays, there is much more emphasis on presentation and style. Lecturing is discouraged because students tend to lose interest and they don't learn much, and I'm not just talking about young people. Even when teaching adults, lessons have to be interactive, and I discovered this while studying for a City and Guilds qualification in Adult and Further Education. We were told that we could lecture for about ten minutes at the most, even when using visual aids such as overhead projections. After that, the students had to be given something to do, for example practical work, role-plays or group discussions. At the very least, we had to stop lecturing at frequent intervals and get the students involved by asking them questions.

The church cannot live in isolation from the world. If people are used to slick presentations at school, or at work, or from the TV, then they also need slick presentations in church, otherwise they get bored. The days are gone, when you could get people into church for a hymn sandwich followed by a sermon. You need to have well-prepared visual aids, and you need to get people involved by organising them to do role-plays and drama. It makes things much more interesting, but it's also a lot of work for the people involved, and it's usually the people who in former days might have gone to the mid-week Bible study. They still go to the same mid-week meeting, but they don't study the Bible any more, and they don't have much time for prayer. Instead they are busy organising drama and presentations for the next Sunday service.

The music has also changed. In the old days they used to have just one person playing an organ, but now it has to be a band with a range of instruments, and a team of worship leaders to bring the congregation in at the right time, and there has to be someone at the back with a mixing unit, making sure that everything balances correctly. Everything is carefully rehearsed at the weekly band practice, by people who would otherwise be at the Bible study, but they haven't got time for that any more because they are too busy doing the music.

The problem is, you have to have the band these days because people have become so accustomed to hearing a full-blown band on TV and at gigs and discos. Back in the 1960's we used to go to a disco on Saturday night and listen to a band, but it was all very new and we didn't really expect to get a band in church on Sunday.

The outcome of all this is that church has had to change. Church attendance has been dwindling steadily for a variety of reasons and I won't go into all of them here. Many churches have closed and the buildings have been demolished or used for other purposes. Those that have survived have done so by creating a style of worship that people find attractive, but they have done so at the cost of their fellowship and spiritual life. In the Evangelical churches that used to preach the Real Gospel, you can't just walk in any more and ask them what they believe. You might get a different response from each member of the congregation, and some of them might be surprised that they are even asked such a question. The consequence of all this is that Evangelical churches have become liberal, not as a matter of choice, but because they are so busy with a multitude of activities, they haven't got time to think about what they believe.

And this brings me back to the parable of the sower that I mentioned on page 86. The church is no longer bearing fruit. Instead, the Word is choked, not by the cares of the world, but by the *cares of the church*, which is just as much of a distraction and in practice it amounts to the same thing.

Home-Based Church

When a church gets out of the habit of regular prayer and Bible study and becomes activity-based, it isn't easy to change it back again. You might get a charismatic leader who can call everybody to order, but it needs to be a real leader who is recognised, and not just an upstart from the congregation.

In most circumstances, it's easier to set up your own meeting in your own home, and while this might appear schismatic, it's actually very Biblical.

> Hear, O Israel: The Lord our God is one Lord: And thou shalt love the Lord thy God with all thine heart, and with all thy soul, and with all thy might. And these words, which I command thee this day, shall be in thine heart: And thou shalt teach them diligently unto thy children, and shalt talk of them when thou sittest in thine house, and when thou walkest by the way, and when thou liest down, and when thou risest up.
>
> *Deut. 6:4-7*

This passage forms part of the Jewish liturgy known as the *Shema*, which means "hear", and Jesus quoted from it when he was asked *"Master, which is the great commandment in the law?"* (Matt. 22:36). He said the greatest commandment was to love God, then he quoted from Lev. 19:18 and said that the second commandment was to love our neighbour.

The Shema contains the instruction to teach the Bible to our children, and to others who come into our homes, and in its most general sense it encourages us to talk about the Bible at every opportunity. Teaching the Bible is part of loving God, and it has to be given high priority.

Notice that the Shema does not tell us to send our children to youth meetings to be taught by others, even though that may be useful. It tells us to teach our children, meaning we are supposed to do it ourselves, and it provides the basis for home-based ministry.

Judaism is home-based to the extent that it is more dependent on the home than the synagogue. There is the weekly Sabbath and various other festivals that are partly home-based and partly synagogue-based, but it's possible to celebrate all the festivals at home if there is no synagogue, and this has sustained the Jews in times of persecution and dispersion. There is actually no need for a synagogue, to practice Judaism, although it's good to have one because it brings the community together.

Christianity, on the other hand, is much more dependent on the church. Of course in its strictest Biblical sense, the word "church" means any informal group of believers meeting together, but for the purpose of this discussion we are talking about an institution with a pastor and elders, and a denominational hierarchy, and usually a church building. Take away the church and Christianity collapses because there is no tradition of home-based meetings. Instead, there are "house groups" which are organised by the church, and to a large extent they follow an agenda that the church has set for them. They might follow a set of study topics, given to them by the church leadership, and they might also have to get involved in the planning and preparation of church services and other activities. The people who live in the houses don't actually have much influence on the house groups. All they do is provide a place to meet.

It would be naïve to suggest that Christians can solve all their problems by emulating the Jews. We all have problems of our own making, and sometimes the Jewish home is not all that it is cracked up to be. However, on the question of home-based meetings it would be good for Christians to take a leaf out of the Jewish book. Christians need to have home-based meetings, organised by the people who live there, for the purpose of teaching the next generation, and discussing the Bible with anyone else who might come. This is the regular practice of the Jews, not only in their homes, but in other places as well. When religious Jews meet each other in the street, they talk about all the usual things such as their families and their work, and then they might talk about the Bible. They feel quite uninhibited about this, and as long as they are free from persecution, they do not feel concerned about becoming known as "Bible bashers".

When Jewish people meet to discuss the Bible, they sometimes run into questions that they can't answer, and from this we get the catch phrase *"Ask the Rabbi"*. If the Rabbi is always being approached by people asking questions, he knows that they are thinking, and there is some useful discussion going on in people's homes, or wherever they might happen to meet.

It's very much the same in churches that encourage people to have their own home-based meetings, provided it's run by the participants themselves, following their own agenda. Questions are discussed in the group and then they might be passed on to the minister or one of the elders if necessary. If the groups are genuinely independent, the questions could be about anything, and there will be a richness and diversity of dialogue that will keep everybody thinking. This type of dialogue is commonplace in Bible-based churches, and it's important to allow the home-based study and discussion to continue, without having a programme imposed on them from above, or allowing the groups to be taken over by the relentless demand for activities. If activities are needed, they should be organised some other way, without encroaching on people's home-based meetings.

Home-Based Church in the New Testament

The early church, for the first few years, was almost entirely Jewish, and it was their custom to meet in houses, although they also had synagogues, and in Jerusalem they had the Temple.

> And they, continuing daily with one accord in the temple, and breaking bread from house to house, did eat their meat with gladness and singleness of heart, Praising God, and having favour with all the people. And the Lord added to the church daily such as should be saved.
>
> *Acts 2:46-47*

When more and more Gentiles came into the church, they also met in houses, and they may have inherited the custom from the Jews, or they might have simply found it the most convenient thing to do.

> Greet Priscilla and Aquila my helpers in Christ Jesus: Who have for my life laid down their own necks: unto whom not only I give thanks, but also all the churches of the Gentiles. Likewise greet the church that is in their house. Salute my well beloved Epaenetus, who is the firstfruits of Achaia unto Christ.
>
> *Rom. 16:3-5*

> Salute the brethren which are in Laodicea, and Nymphas, and the church which is in his house.
>
> *Col. 4:15*

> And to our beloved Apphia, and Archippus our fellowsoldier, and to the church in thy house:
>
> *Philemon 2*

There is actually no specific mention of a church building in the New Testament. Even when we have a phrase such as the *"house of God"*, it means a spiritual community, not a building.

> But if I tarry long, that thou mayest know how thou oughtest to behave thyself in the house of God, which is the church of the living God, the pillar and ground of the truth.
>
> *1 Tim. 3:15*

Clearly, as the church grew, there must have been a need for places where large numbers of people could meet, but there is no obvious evidence of church buildings. In that case, if nobody had a house that was big enough, they must have met in any available building.

The Spiritual Community

At this point it becomes obvious that "church" is not a building. It's a community of believers who meet together regularly for prayer, worship and study.

Neither can it be fully defined by an institutional hierarchy consisting of pastors, elders, and denominational moderators, although these structures are useful because they preserve continuity and help the church to have a visible presence.

The real definition of the church is any group of believers who meet together for spiritual worship, anytime, anywhere, in either a formal or informal situation.

I have found, and there are many people who will concur with this, that the real life of the church is in the unregulated home-based group. This is where we find out what the Real Gospel consists of, and we can question each other's views about creation, the fall, salvation, baptism, the resurrection of the dead, the return of the Lord, and anything else that makes up our basis of faith. This is where new believers can be counselled and brought to a full understanding of the faith, so that they can gain confidence and participate in discussions with other believers. This is the place where mature believers can bring their treasures out of their storehouses, both the old and the new. This is where strange and unfamiliar doctrines can be evaluated, and if necessary denounced as heresies, and in any healthy home-based group, the Pseudo-Gospel described in Chapter 2 would not survive for very long.

So, in our quest for the Real Gospel, we first have to find the Real Church, unless we want to do it ourselves which can be a rather lonely and isolated experience. I have found that the best forum for this type of study is the independent home-based group, meeting with or without the active support of a more formal, structured organisation called "church".

Appendix 1 - The Philosophy of Evolution

We've heard it all so many times, haven't we? "Evolution is true, it's a proven fact". But it isn't proved, and it isn't a fact, because such a thing is beyond the capabilities of science.

Science is about the observation and interpretation of the world around us, and is subject to the following limitations:

- We can only observe the world as it is now. Even when we observe data that we reasonably believe to represent the past, such as tree rings and distant starlight, we are still making our observations in real time, in the present.

- There can be multiple interpretations of all our observations. For example, we know that beneath our feet, almost everywhere in the world, there are many fossils, the impressions of dead plants and animals, embedded in the rocks, and sometimes they are arranged in distinct layers with different types of fossil in each layer. Some scientists call it the geologic column, laid down slowly over millions of years of evolution. Others call it flood sediment, laid down quickly during the global flood, and stratified as a consequence of fluid dynamics, and they consider the distribution of fossils to be dependent on the mobility of animals while still alive.

Even in cases where we have only one reasonable interpretation of the data, we still have to consider the possibility that new interpretations might emerge which are just as reasonable.

One of the most difficult tasks of science is to find out about the past. You can't observe the past, you can only observe the present, but you can try and extrapolate your data so that it extends into the past, if you know something about how the data changes with time. However, it's a hazardous journey because the further back you try to go, the more you are prone to error. For example, if you are measuring the decay rates of radioactive substances, you have to make assumptions about what the substance was like at a time in the distant past, when the physical conditions might not be the same as they are now, and you have to be sure that the substances you are measuring really are decay products and are not just substances that happen to be there for other reasons.

You also have to make some assumptions about age before you start the measurement process. For example, carbon dating[32] measures thousands of years, but the potassium-argon[33] method measures millions of years, or so it is supposed. When you take a sample for testing, you have to use the appropriate method because the instruments are calibrated for the appropriate timescale. This leads to some strange anomalies, because if you take a dinosaur bone to a carbon dating laboratory, and you tell them it's a dinosaur bone, they won't date it because it's too old. However, if you don't tell them, they will do the test and give you a result in thousands of years, and then you can embarrass them by telling them it's a dinosaur bone. Conversely, there have been people who took samples of volcanic rock that are known to be less than 50 years old, because they knew about the eruptions that had occurred in the recent history of the area. They had the samples tested, using the potassium-argon method, and got results as high as 3.5 million years.[34] Obviously it's ridiculous if you have to know the approximate age of something before you test it. You are supposed to use the test to find out the age.

Similar anomalies and false assumptions occur with the dating of fossils. You can go to a museum, where you are told that a fossil is

---

[32] We all absorb radioactive carbon-14 from the atmosphere during our lifetime which decays to carbon-12 after we are dead.

[33] Igneous and volcanic rocks can be dated from radioactive potassium-40 which decays to argon-40. Sedimentary rocks can sometimes be dated using this method, if there is potassium in their cementation products.

[34] Snelling, A., *Radioactive 'dating' failure*, Answers in Genesis, Creation, 22(1), Dec. 1999 - Feb. 2000, pp.18-21. <www.answersingenesis.org/home/area/magazines/docs/cenv22n1_dating_failure.asp>, March 2004.

so many millions of years old, because it comes from a particular stratum in the geologic column. Then when you ask how they date the geologic column, they say they date it from the fossils. So the reasoning is circular. You date the fossils from the rocks, and the rocks from the fossils.

The problem is, rocks don't come with labels on them saying "I am so many millions of years old", and if you really don't know the age of something, it's better just to come clean and say you don't know.

There is one area of science where we know we are working with long timescales, and this is in astronomy. The universe is very big, and it takes a long time for starlight to arrive from distant galaxies, but we also know that space and time can throw up some strange anomalies, and I will deal with some of these in Appendix 4.

The Philosophical Divide

In the field of creation and evolution, people tend to become polarised as a consequence of a philosophical viewpoint. An atheist will tend to go for the geologic column, because it involves a long timescale, suitable for the evolution. A Christian, or someone who otherwise believes in Biblical history, would go for the flood sediment theory.

The interpretation of data, according the philosophical viewpoints, is summarised as follows:

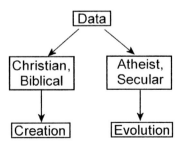

Within this philosophical divide, there is, unfortunately, a fair amount of abuse coming from the evolutionist side. They talk about *real scientists*, meaning themselves, and *creation "scientists"*, meaning the Christians who don't deserve to be called scientists, so they always use the quotation marks.

Among the creation "scientists" we have the following famous names.

- Isaac Newton, who discovered the laws of motion and defined the rules of calculus. He is well known for his science, but he also took a very keen interest in ancient history and Biblical chronology.[35]

- Johann Kepler, who defined the mathematical rules of planetary motion.

- Michael Faraday, who discovered electro-magnetics.

- James Clerk Maxwell, who discovered the laws of statistical thermodynamics.

- Louis Pasteur, who provided the foundation of bacteriology.

These are just a few of the great scientists of the past who believed in creation. There are many more of them, listed by Henry Morris,[36] and the list includes people who lived both before and after Darwin, opposing the evolutionary theories of their time.

Creationists are often accused of manipulating the data to fit a religious viewpoint. We are told that we should just observe the data and find out what it means, without trying to make it fit into a Biblical creation scenario. To this, we have to respond that evolutionists are manipulating the data, because they flatly deny that there is any design in nature when it is staring them in the face. Even the common mousetrap has to be designed, yet they deny the existence of design in living organisms that are so much more complex.

---

[35] Manuel, Frank, *Isaac Newton: Historian*.

[36] Morris, Henry, *Bible-Believing Scientists of the Past*, Institute for Creation Research, Impact Paper 103, January 1982.
<http://www.icr.org/pubs/imp/imp-103.htm>, March 2004.

Greek Philosophy

Although Darwin is commonly credited as the founder of the modern theory of evolution, he was actually building on a much earlier foundation that was laid by the ancient Greeks.

Our knowledge of the early philosophers comes primarily from Aristotle (384-322 BC) who was a student at the Academy of Plato in Athens, and then began lecturing. In his Metaphysics[37], he discusses observation, memory and intelligence and says that the greatest wisdom comes not from the observations themselves, but from the understanding of their causes. He says that most of the early philosophers considered material principles to be the primary causes of all things, and matter might change from one form to another, but there is a primary entity that always persists. He credits Thales[38] of Miletus (c.625-546 BC) as the founder of this school of philosophy, who said that the permanent entity is water, on the basis that the seeds and nutriment of everything is moist, and suggested that the earth floats on water. Aristotle goes on to say that there are some people who think that this view of the primary entity is probably very ancient and might be based on Oceanus and Tethys, the parents of creation, and the oath of the gods which was believed to be by water, known as the Styx. Aristotle was uncertain about whether this was really an ancient view, although this is not surprising considering that the Greeks knew very little of their own ancient history, and borrowed it from the legends of other nations, especially the Egyptians, adapting it to suit themselves, a matter that is discussed in detail by Jacob Bryant.[39]

Plutarch (AD c.46 - c.122) studied at the academy in Athens that had been founded by Plato, and then later in life he returned to his home town of Chaeronea in Boeotia, a province of Greece to the

---

[37] Tredennick, Hugh, *Aristotle: Metaphysics.*
For details of early philosophers see Book I, para. 983b-984a,
<www.non-contradiction.com/ac_works_b37.asp>.
[38] Thales corresponds to the Greek *Thalasa*, which means water, so it seems that Thales was so named because of his philosophy.
[39] Bryant, Jacob, *A New System or an Analysis of Ancient Mythology*, vol. 3.

north of the Gulf of Corinth. He wrote many books, mostly biographies, and he also wrote a collection called the *Moralia* (Moral Writings), including *Isis and Osiris* which gives an account of the mythology of Egypt. He describes the Egyptian view of origins, and the Greek habit of copying their mythology, as follows:[40]

> They say that the sun and moon do not use chariots, but boats in which to sail round in their courses; and by this they intimate that the nourishment and origin of these heavenly bodies is from moisture. They think also that Homer, like Thales, had gained his knowledge from the Egyptians, when he postulated water as the source and origin of all things; for, according to them, Oceanus is Osiris, and Tethys is Isis, since she is the kindly nurse and provider for all things.

In the same book, Plutarch gives us evidence that Osiris was styled on Noah, since he was shut away in a chest and put to sea, and although the substance of the story is quite different from the story of Noah, the two accounts have a number of common details. The passage from Plutarch, together with some important context about the calendar, is as follows:[41]

> They say that the Sun, when he became aware of Rhea's intercourse with Cronus, invoked a curse upon her that she should not give birth to a child in any month or year; but Hermes, being enamoured of the goddess, consorted with her. Later, playing at draughts with the moon, he won from her the seventieth part of each of her periods of illumination, and from all the winnings he composed five days, and intercalated them as an addition to the three hundred and sixty days. The Egyptians even now call these five days intercalated and celebrate them as the birthdays of the gods. They relate that on the first of these days Osiris was born, ... On the second of these days Arueris was born whom they call Apollo, and some call him also the elder Horus. On the

---

[40] Babbitt, F. C., *Plutarch: Moralia,* Vol. V, Loeb Classical Library, 1936. This quotation is from *Isis and Osiris*, para. 364c-d.
<www.ukans.edu/history/index/europe/ancient_rome/E/Roman/Texts/Plutarch/Moralia/Isis_and_Osiris*/B.html>.
[41] Babbitt, F.C., *Plutarch, Moralia, Isis and Osiris*, para. 355d-356d.

third day Typhon was born, but not in due season or manner, but with a blow he broke through his mother's side and leapt forth. On the fourth day Isis was born in the regions that are ever moist; and on the fifth Nephthys, to whom they give the name of Finality and the name of Aphrodite, and some also the name of Victory. ...

One of the first acts related of Osiris in his reign was to deliver the Egyptians from their destitute and brutish manner of living. This he did by showing them the fruits of cultivation, by giving them laws, and by teaching them to honour the gods. Later he travelled over the whole earth civilizing it without the slightest need of arms, but most of the peoples he won over to his way by the charm of his persuasive discourse combined with song and all manner of music. Hence the Greeks came to identify him with Dionysus.

During his absence the tradition is that Typhon attempted nothing revolutionary because Isis, who was in control, was vigilant and alert; but when he returned home Typhon contrived a treacherous plot against him and formed a group of conspirators seventy-two in number. He had also the co-operation of a queen from Ethiopia who was there at the time and whose name they report as Aso. Typhon, having secretly measured Osiris's body and having made ready a beautiful chest of corresponding size artistically ornamented, caused it to be brought into the room where the festivity was in progress. The company was much pleased at the sight of it and admired it greatly, whereupon Typhon jestingly promised to present it to the man who should find the chest to be exactly his length when he lay down in it. They all tried it in turn, but no one fitted it; then Osiris got into it and lay down, and those who were in the plot ran to it and slammed down the lid, which they fastened by nails from the outside and also by using molten lead. Then they carried the chest to the river and sent it on its way to the sea through the Tanitic Mouth. Wherefore the Egyptians even to this day name this mouth the hateful and execrable. Such is the tradition. They say also that the date on which this deed was done was the seventeenth day of Athyr, when the sun passes through Scorpion, and in the twenty-eighth year of the reign of Osiris; but some say that these are the years of his life and not of his reign.

This passage uses the Greek word *larnax* to describe the chest in which Osiris was confined, and this is the very same word that is used by Apollodorus[42] when he tells the story of Deucalion and his wife Pyrrha, who escaped from a flood in Attica by floating a chest. Deucalion is widely believed to be the Greek Noah, although the flood that he survived was probably a later event. The common details that match the story of Osiris with Noah are as follows:

- There is a description of the activities of Osiris, during his reign, ending with the statement that the Greeks identified him with Dionysus. This character is known in Greek mythology as the god of pleasure who gives out wine.[43] We also know that Noah cultivated grapes and made wine, after his survival of the Flood.

- The chest in which Osiris was confined was constructed according to exact measurements, as was the ark of Noah.

- Osiris went into the chest voluntarily, without being forced, just as Noah went voluntarily into the ark.

- Osiris was shut in, as soon as he got into the chest. Noah was also shut into the ark, because the Lord closed the door. Noah did not close it himself.

- The chest was put into the river and drifted out to sea, just as the ark floated on water.

- Osiris got into the chest on the seventeenth day of the month of Athyr, just as Noah went into the ark and the Flood began on the seventeenth day of the second month.

This last point is the most dramatic of all. Not only does the same day of the month appear in the two stories, but it was also the same time of the year, and this is why I have included the calendar information in the quotation from Plutarch.

---

[42] Frazer, J. G., (editor), *Apollodorus: The Library*, 1.7.2.
<www.perseus.tufts.edu/cgi-bin/ptext?lookup=Apollod.+1.7.2>.
[43] Greek Mythology Link, Dionysus,
<http://homepage.mac.com/cparada/GML/Dionysus2.html>.

The Philosophy of Evolution

The Egyptian civil calendar consisted of twelve months of thirty days each, making up 360 days. To these were added five extra days which were festivals to celebrate the birthdays of the gods, and the Greeks referred to these as the epagomenal days. The year began when the star Sirius (Sothis) appeared above the horizon, just in advance of the sunrise, an event known as the heliacal rising of Sirius. This occurred regularly at about the time of the summer solstice, when the Nile began to rise and became flooded. However, there was a problem with the calendar because it consisted of 365 days altogether and missed out the quarter day that would be needed to keep it in line with the seasons. This caused the calendar to drift backwards so that New Year (1st Thoth) would occur one day earlier every four years, and would eventually go round a complete cycle and return to its starting point. This would take 1461 years of 365 days, which would correspond to 1460 solar years of 365.25 days. This period is known as the "Sothic cycle". For a long time there was no attempt to correct the calendar, and they simply allowed it to drift, but for agricultural purposes they used the heliacal rising of Sirius to mark the beginning of the seasons.

The second month in the year was Phaophi and the third was Athyr, the month when Osiris was shut into the chest. Of course this could be at any season, depending on how the calendar had drifted, so how can we know when it happened? An important clue is in the text from Plutarch because he says *"the seventeenth day of Athyr, when the sun passes through Scorpion"*. We know that the sun is in Scorpio from 24th October to 22nd November, and it is during this period that Noah must have entered the ark.

Moses described the event using the Babylonian calendar which is luni-solar, and has twelve lunar months in some years and thirteen in others, on the basis of a 19-year cycle that has 235 lunar months. The Jewish calendar used today is based on the same Babylonian system, and the New Year (Rosh Hashana) jumps forward and backward, depending on whether or not the previous year contained a thirteenth month. The average date for New Year is 20th September, using a rough calculation from a number of successive years, but it varies by about two weeks around that average. In that case, the average date for the 17th day of the second month would be

113

6th November, and it would vary between 23rd October and 20th November, which matches very closely the period of Scorpio.

This gives us the result that Osiris was confined to the chest at the same time of the year when Noah entered the ark. The Egyptian month of Athyr must have corresponded to the second month of the Hebrew (Babylonian) calendar, so that Osiris and Noah both went into their respective confinements on the seventeenth day of the same month.

Taking all of the matching details together, we can be in no doubt that the confinement of Osiris is a distorted version of the story of Noah.

Although the details are similar, the substance of the two stories is actually quite different. The chest in which Osiris was confined was a coffin, probably of the type that was used for Egyptian mummies. The lid was nailed down and sealed with lead so that Osiris would die from suffocation. The ark, on the other hand, was for the preservation of life, so that Noah and his family could survive the Flood. To understand how they match up, we have to continue with the story of Osiris, as it is related by Plutarch.

When Isis heard what had happened to Osiris, she went in search of the coffin and found that it had come ashore near the land of Byblus,[44] and it was enclosed in a great tree that had grown around it. The king of that country had cut the tree down and used it as a pillar to hold up the roof of his palace. She went to the palace to ask for the tree, and having gained their consent she removed it and stripped away the wood to reveal the coffin. She put the coffin on a boat and took it to Egypt, where she opened it and wept over the body of her husband. Then she left it hidden in a secure place and went off to see her infant son Horus, who was being looked after in Buto.[45]

To avoid confusion, some explanation is needed at this point, because there are two versions of the god called Horus. There is Horus the elder, already mentioned as one of the five gods who were

---

[44] Jebeil (Gebal) on the coast of Lebanon, about 20 miles north of Beirut.
[45] Most likely Tell el-Farein on the Nile delta, about 60 miles east of Alexandria.

born on the days that were added to the year. This Horus was the brother of Osiris. Horus the younger, otherwise called Harpocrates, was born as the posthumous son of Isis and Osiris, and this is the child who was being looked after in Buto.

While Isis was away, Typhon found the coffin and cut the body of Osiris into fourteen pieces and scattered them in different places. When Isis heard of it, she went in search of the pieces and held a funeral for each piece that she found. Some time later, Osiris came from the place of the dead, to give his son Horus some military training so that he could succeed him as king.

Typhon accused Horus of being an illegitimate child, in an attempt to deprive him of his succession to the kingdom, but Hermes (the Greek counterpart of the Egyptian Thoth) pleaded his cause and the gods decided that he was legitimate. Osiris had consorted with Isis after his death, and Harpocrates (Horus) was born.

This story, as related by Plutarch, implies that Horus was conceived from the body of Osiris on the journey back to Egypt, although it is not specifically stated that this is the case. This would create a problem with the timing of his birth, because he was in Buto, being looked after by someone else, so he was obviously born before the journey. Perhaps Osiris had come back from the dead sometime earlier and consorted with Isis. This apparent uncertainty about the timing of the birth of Horus might have been the basis on which Typhon claimed his illegitimacy. The decision of the gods was that Isis and Osiris managed to get together somehow, although we know neither how nor when.

The mysterious birth of Horus, as the successor to Osiris, was important for the Egyptians because it represented rebirth and regeneration, and Plutarch explains how it is related to the agriculture of the Nile region as follows:[46]

> As they regard the Nile as the effusion of Osiris, so they hold and believe the earth to be the body of Isis, not all of it, but so much of it as

---

[46] Babbitt, F. C, *Plutarch: Moralia, Isis and Osiris*, para. 366a.
<www.ukans.edu/history/index/europe/ancient_rome/E/Roman/Texts/
Plutarch/Moralia/Isis_and_Osiris*/B.html>.

the Nile covers, fertilizing it and uniting with it. From this union they make Horus to be born. The all-conserving and fostering Hora, that is the seasonable tempering of the surrounding air, is Horus, who they say was brought up by Leto in the marshes round about Buto; for the watery and saturated land best nurtures those exhalations which quench and abate aridity and dryness.

For agricultural purposes, the Egyptians had three seasons in the year, of four months each. The first was the inundation, when the Nile became flooded, and this began approximately at the heliacal rising of Sirius. The second season was the winter, when the waters had receded leaving the damp soil, and this was the time for planting crops. The third season was the summer, which was the time for harvesting. This cycle was essential to the prosperity of Egypt, and it was represented in their mythology. The inundation, represented by Osiris, was considered to be a state of death when nothing was possible, but in death the conditions for new life were being prepared as the land, represented by Isis, was watered. When the waters had receded, the land was in perfect condition for planting crops so that new life was possible, represented by Horus.

At this point we see the similarity between the stories of Noah and Osiris, in substance and not just in detail. When Noah and his family were in the ark, the world was in the process of destruction, and in all probability the light from the sun was totally obscured. They lived in darkness, except for any lights that they could kindle for themselves. It must have been like a state of death, where they could do nothing, and the animals were in hibernation. Then when the Flood came to an end, and the waters receded, they emerged to new life and repopulated the world. The ark was the vessel that contained the seeds of regeneration, and Noah was like Osiris going into the ark, but more like Horus when he came out.

There is a lot more that could be said about this subject, and it is discussed in detail by Bryant, but at this point, we need to return to the reasons why we got started on it. We began this section by discussing Thales, who believed that everything came from water, and there were some who believed that the primary entity was associated with Oceanus and Tethys, the gods of the sea. Plutarch identified these people as the Egyptians, and he says that Oceanus and Tethys were derived from Osiris and Isis. We have seen, from our discussion of the mythology of Egypt, that Osiris and Isis are styled on Noah and his wife, and in that case, the primary entity is not water in any general sense, but the survival of Noah and his family from the waters of the Flood. The ancient view of water as the primary entity is a distortion of the story of the Flood, as Noah and his wife were turned into the gods of water, first by the Egyptians and then by the Greeks.

After discussing Thales, Aristotle continues with some of the other philosophers.[47] Anaximenes[48] and Diogenes[49] believed that air was the first principle. Hippassus[50] and Heraclitus[51] believed it was fire. Empedocles[52] added earth and said there are four first principles altogether, water, air, fire and earth. Anaxagoras[53] said there are an infinite number of first principles, and matter could be generated and destroyed by combination and differentiation, but otherwise it existed permanently. Thus it appears that he defined a very early principle of conservation of matter.

At this stage, people began to argue about how it was possible for generation and destruction to occur out of one or more entities, and what was the cause of change. Parmenides[54] suggested that change could occur because of the existence of opposites such as hot and cold, and the kinetic nature of fire which was different from

---

[47] Aristotle, *Metaphysics*, Book I, continuing from para. 984a. <www.non-contradiction.com/ac_works_b37.asp>.

[48] Anaximenes of Miletus, (d.528BC). Student of Anaximander who was a younger contemporary of Thales.

[49] Diogenes of Apollonia in Crete. Student of Anaximenes.

[50] Hippasus of Metapontum (fl. 5th cent. BC). Pythagorean philosopher and mathematician.

[51] Heraclitus of Ephesus (late 6th cent. BC). Ephesus was near Miletus, the home base of Thales and many other philosophers.

[52] Empedocles (fl. 450BC). Citizen of Agrigentum in Sicily but went to Thourioi in southern Italy.

[53] Anaxagoras of Clazomenae in Asia Minor (c.500-428BC).

[54] Parmenides of Elea in southern Italy (b. 510BC).

water and earth. Thus we have a view that resembles the Second Law of Thermodynamics, which defines the distribution of energy, a subject that is discussed in Appendix 3.

However, they were baffled by the question of how it was possible for primary elements such as fire and earth to generate all the complexities of nature, by spontaneity and chance. Some people, including Anaxagoras and Hermotimus,[55] took the view that there must be Mind in nature. Thus we have a view that is similar to Creationism, or its modern secular counterpart, Intelligent Design. Empedocles took into account that nature includes not just order and beauty, but also disorder and ugliness. Another unnamed philosopher introduced Love and Strife as their respective causes, although Empedocles himself can be credited with this because, in the opinion of Aristotle, he recognised good and evil as first principles.

Aristotle continues his discussion with the remark that these philosophers, as far as Empedocles, seem to have identified in a vague sense two primary causes, the material cause and the cause of motion. However, he criticises Anaxagoras for using Mind as an artificial device for producing order, as a last resort when he feels that he must get a meaningful result, and he would much rather use other causes if he could find them. Thus we have the Greek version of a popular complaint against creationists, that we insert God into our arguments when science cannot explain something. Of course this is not the way that creationists think of God, but some evolutionists would like to think that we do.

The Greek philosophy of origins appears to have gone in three phases:

- Phase 1 was the identification of material entities as primary causes, including water, air, earth and fire. The notion of water as the primary cause was tied up with ancient mythology, derived from the story of the Flood, regardless of whether Thales intended it that way. Air and fire also appeared in mythology, as

---

[55] Hermotimus of Clazomenae. A contemporary of Anaxagoras and thought by some to be his tutor although it cannot be proved.

Zeus hurled his thunderbolts from the sky (a matter that will be discussed in Appendix 2 in association with modern attempts to create life). Earth appeared in mythology as Gaia the earth goddess, and her Egyptian counterpart Isis who produced life from the Nile, the effluent of Osiris. It is impossible to imagine that the early philosophers came up with the notions of water, air, earth and fire as the primary entities, without being influenced in some way by the mythologies that exerted a powerful influence on the societies in which they lived. Even if they had discarded the mythologies from their own minds, they could not have discarded it from public discussion. Ideas are always more persistent, and more easily distributed, when they are associated with popular myths.

• Phase 2 was an attempt to define generation and destruction of material entities, and to define causes for change, in a way that became increasingly secular, so that the old mythologies were discarded as irrelevant to the theory of origins. This had some positive results, giving Greek versions of the laws of conservation of matter, and distribution of energy, although it failed to explain the existence of complex order.

• Phase 3 was the introduction of Mind as a primary cause, because of the observation that complex order does not come into existence from causes that are based on chance. It was this phase of Greek philosophy that the Apostle Paul was referring to, when he claimed that the Greeks had observed the work of God in nature:

For the invisible things of him from the creation of the world are clearly seen, being understood by the things that are made, even his eternal power and Godhead; so that they are without excuse: because that, when they knew God, they glorified him not as God, neither were thankful; but became vain in their imaginations, and their foolish heart was darkened. Professing themselves to be wise, they became fools, and changed the glory of the uncorruptible God into an image made like to corruptible man, and to birds, and fourfooted beasts, and creeping things.

Rom. 1:20-23

119

The tragedy was, that for many of the Greeks, the existence of a Creator was just an intellectual exercise. Instead of worshipping him, they went back to the old mythologies, worshipping idols in the form of both men and beasts.

History always repeats itself, because people never take the trouble to learn from the successes and failures of their predecessors. Modern science, for the most part, is currently in phase 2 of the Greek philosophy, where life is supposed to have emerged from a watery primeval soup, and an atmosphere that was zapped by thunderbolts from the sky, and in the process of time, life crawled out of the sea and emerged onto dry land.

There are, of course, many people who are in phase 3, either because they have always been there, or because they have been persuaded by the arguments of creation science that there must be design in nature. However, it hasn't yet reached the stage where taxpayer's money gets spent on creation research. If it ever does, every religion, both ancient and modern, will be competing for public funds.

Appendix 2 - The Impossibility of Chemical Evolution

The Stanley Miller Experiment – Life from Electricity?

Erasmus Darwin, the grandfather of Charles Darwin, thought that inanimate matter could be jerked into life using electricity. He was the inspiration of Mary Shelley's story of Frankenstein, and the idea of the electric spark of life was quite popular at the time. It was probably derived from Greek mythology, where Persephone (Cura) made a man out of clay, and Zeus gave him life. The Latin author Hyginus[56] is credited with preserving a fragment of this tale, and he used the word *spiritus* which means *breath of life*. However, since Zeus is well known as the sky god with a thunderbolt in his hand, it could easily have been modified so that the *spark of life* becomes a variation of the theme.

In 1953 there was great enthusiasm over an experiment performed by Stanley Miller, when he produced amino acids from a mixture of gases consisting of methane, hydrogen, ammonia and water vapour. He passed the gas mixture through a large glass bulb where they were subjected to an electrical discharge of 60,000 volts between a pair of electrodes. This had no observable effect over a short period, but after about a week a tarry substance began to appear. The products of the reaction were condensed out and were found to contain small amounts of the amino acids glycine ($NH_2.CH_2.COOH$) and alanine ($NH_2.CH(CH_3)COOH$).

---

[56] Gaius Julius Hyginus, 1st century AD Latin author, and student of Alexander Polyhistor. The story of Persephone (Cura) and the creation of man is from Fabulae (Fables), 220. This is attributed to Hyginus as a compilation from earlier fragments, although it might have been done by another unknown author. For the Latin text and translation, see Loyola University, Department of Classical Studies, <www.loyno.edu/~wemajor/coursestuff/texts/hyg220.htm>.

This experiment was widely acclaimed to be a laboratory simulation of the beginnings of life in the atmosphere of the primeval soup. His gas mixture might not suit everybody's choice, and it is now thought that the so-called primeval atmosphere was made up of carbon dioxide, nitrogen, water and small amounts of hydrogen, although this does not diminish the significance of his experiment. He showed that amino acids can be produced from commonly available gases, and this was a major achievement. However, it takes a lot more than amino acids to create life, as we shall see.

Amino Acids and Proteins

Amino acids have the following general formula:

$$NH_2-\underset{\underset{H}{|}}{\overset{\overset{R}{|}}{C}}-COOH$$

The radical "R" can be any combination of C, H, O and N, including benzene rings. The two simplest amino acids are:

Glycine (R = H)
Alanine (R = CH_3)

Amino acids are both acid and alkali at the same time. The amine group (NH_2) at one end gives off a hydrogen ion and the carboxyl group (COOH) at the other end gives off a hydroxyl ion.

$$NH_2-\underset{\underset{H}{|}}{\overset{\overset{R_1}{|}}{C}}-\underset{\overset{||}{O}}{C}\!-\!OH \qquad H\!-\!N\!-\!\underset{\underset{H}{|}}{\overset{\overset{H\ \ R_2}{|\ \ |}}{C}}-COOH$$

After the loss of a water molecule, the remaining components are capable of joining together in a bond known as the peptide bond as follows:

$$NH_2-\underset{\underset{H}{|}}{\overset{\overset{R_1}{|}}{C}}-\underset{\underset{O}{\parallel}}{\overset{\overset{}{}}{C}}-\underset{}{\overset{\overset{H}{|}}{N}}-\underset{\underset{H}{|}}{\overset{\overset{R_2}{|}}{C}}-COOH$$

Peptide
Bond

This example of two amino acids joining together is called a dipeptide. It has an amino group at one end, and a carboxyl group at the other end, the same as its component amino acids. The chain can be extended to any length, and there can be any combination of radicals R_1, R_2 etc., in sequence along the chain. When long chains are formed, with different radicals in sequence, they are called proteins.

The peptide bond is very difficult to form under purely synthetic conditions where there are no biological substances present. Even the simplest dipeptides require long and tortuous reaction paths involving many intermediate stages, so that the formation of the long chains that make up proteins becomes impossible. However, proteins are formed easily in the presence of enzymes, which are catalytic proteins. This creates a problem for evolution, because you need proteins to make proteins, and there is no starting point.

A second problem for evolution is the language of proteins. There are 23 different radicals (R_1, R_2, ... R_{23}) in the proteins found in nature, and they are arranged in meaningful sequences along the protein chains. They are the characters of an alphabet which makes up words and sentences, telling the protein what it is supposed to do.

The question is, how did this come about? Language can only exist when it is spoken or written by somebody who knows what it means, so we get an opportunity for some philosophical debate on the words *"And God said..."* (Gen. 1:20) and *"In the beginning was the Word"* (John 1:1).

DNA and Base Pair Sequences

Although it is possible to join amino acids together in the presence of enzymes to make proteins, this process in itself is insufficient to maintain the coded sequences that are essential for life. Proteins do not replicate themselves, therefore other agents are required to produce multiple occurrences of the same protein molecules with identical coded sequences. The agent that holds the key to the coded information needs to be able to replicate itself, so that it can provide the same information to every cell of a living organism.

This agent is called deoxy-ribo-nucleic acid, otherwise known as DNA. It is the largest of all molecules found in nature, and has the shape of a ladder that has been bent over and then twisted to form a double helix.

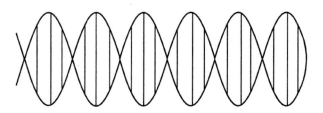

The rungs of the ladder are made up of "base pairs" as follows:

Adenine joins to Thymine (A-T)
Guanine joins to Cytosine (G-C)

Working along either of the two legs of the ladder, we have the bases A, T, G, C in any combination, each matched to its complementary base on the other leg.

Straightening out the ladder for simplicity we have:

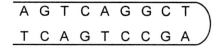

A	G	T	C	A	G	G	C	T
T	C	A	G	T	C	C	G	A

DNA Replication

During cell replication, the double helix uncoils itself and straightens out, breaking the weak hydrogen bonds that hold the pairs together.

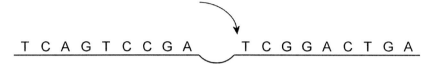

T C A G T C C G A   T C G G A C T G A

Then another leg forms alongside it, with a set of complementary bases, so there is a new ladder, twice as long as the original one.

A G T C A G G C T	A G C C T G A C T
T C A G T C C G A	T C G G A C T G A

Then the ladder is cut in half and the ends are closed off, so you have two molecules of DNA, each with a sequence of base pairs identical to the original one. (Take the one on the right, turn it round 180° and you will see that it is identical to the one on the left).

A G T C A G G C T	A G C C T G A C T
T C A G T C C G A	T C G G A C T G A

Finally each of the new DNA molecules coils up to form a double helix.

Translating the Code from DNA to Protein

The sequence of bases along any leg of the DNA molecule forms a set of instructions, in a language made up of meaningful words and sentences. But the alphabet of the DNA language has only four characters, so how does it translate into the 23 characters used by proteins? The answer is that three characters of the DNA alphabet are used to make up one character of the protein alphabet, so for example you might have:

$TCA = R_1$
$GTC = R_2$
etc.

125

The number of possible combinations is 4 × 4 × 4 = 64, which is more than enough to code for all the proteins.

This is a very efficient method of storing all the genetic code of an organism, using the fewest possible characters. It can be compared with computer coded information which uses only two values, zero and one, but arranges them in combinations of eight, called "bytes", to make up all the characters and symbols of the computer keyboard.

No computer programmer could fail to be impressed with the method of coding the information in the DNA and translating it to proteins. We couldn't have done it better ourselves and we have to admire the work of the Creator.

Cell Structure

Before we study the transport mechanism that enables information to be transferred from DNA to proteins, we have to study the structure of the cell.

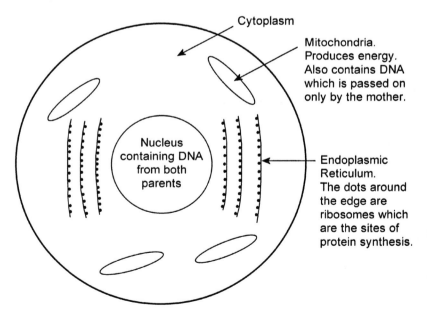

Cytoplasm

Mitochondria.
Produces energy.
Also contains DNA
which is passed on
only by the mother.

Nucleus
containing DNA
from both
parents

Endoplasmic
Reticulum.
The dots around
the edge are
ribosomes which
are the sites of
protein synthesis.

Each cell is made up of a nucleus surrounded by a cytoplasm. The DNA, containing a mixture of genes from both the mother and father, is on the chromosomes within the nucleus. Within the cytoplasm there are energy-producing regions called mitochondria, where there is additional DNA with gene sequences contributed only by the mother.

Proteins are formed on the surface of small granules called ribosomes, in a region of the cytoplasm called the endoplasmic reticulum.

RNA Transport Mechanisms

During the manufacture of proteins, genetic information has to be transferred from the DNA in the nucleus to the ribosomes in the cytoplasm. This is achieved using another large molecule called ribo-nucleic acid, or RNA. This has base pairs, similar to DNA, but it has uracil instead of thymine, so we have:

Adenine joins to Uracil (A-U)
Guanine joins to Cytosine (G-C)

There are two different types of RNA, known as messenger RNA and transfer RNA.

Messenger RNA has a single strand of unpaired bases which line up along one of the legs of a DNA molecule. Each base on the RNA is complementary to a base on the DNA.

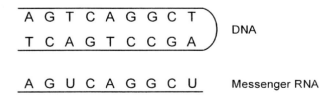

127

Transfer RNA is a short double helix with base pairs along its length, but with unpaired bases at both ends as follows:

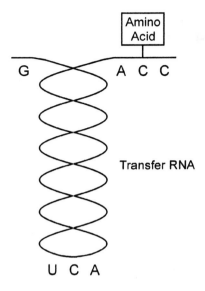

- There are three bases at the closed end which could be any combination of A, U, G and C, and they associate the transfer RNA with a specific amino acid.

- There are four bases ACC and G at the open end. ACC acts as a hook which attaches to the amino acid molecule.

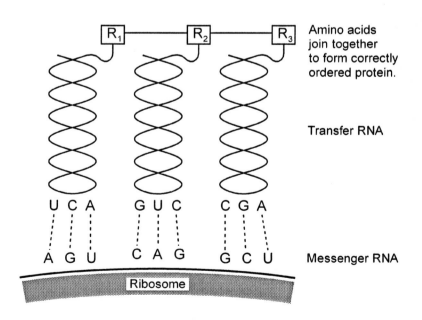

The messenger RNA moves out of the nucleus and into the cytoplasm, where it attaches itself to a ribosome.

The transfer RNA molecules find their way to the ribosomes, and position themselves so that the three bases at the closed end become attached to the complementary sequence of bases on the messenger RNA.

The amino acids, with their radicals R_1, R_2, R_3 etc. become lined up in the correct order and join themselves up to make a protein. Thus, the genetic information from the DNA has been transferred to the protein, using the messenger RNA and transfer RNA as the transport mechanism.

Perfect from the Beginning

All living organisms have DNA molecules with coded information which tells them how they should function. They all use the same transport mechanisms, so that the information is translated from one alphabet to another and written into the proteins. Plants and animals have different cell structures, but the method of storing and processing genetic information is the same.

Any disruption of the genetic sequence can have adverse consequences, causing cancer, deformity and genetic diseases. We know very well that people who are perfectly healthy can get cancer from radioactivity, toxic substances and too much sunlight. Gene sequences are disrupted and defective cells are produced. If cell replication is triggered, the cancer becomes malignant and there is a growing tumour which can be life-threatening.

With this in mind, what are we to make of a genetic information system that has to evolve? At best, it would start off with wrong information that causes cancer. If it was capable of producing proteins at all, most of them would be configured wrongly and would have to be destroyed, and then there has to be an immune system to destroy them. But evolution has been spared all of that, because we have already seen that there is no chemical mechanism for the formation of the first proteins from ordinary chemicals, or the first DNA, or the first RNA.

We have to conclude that there was no evolution, because there is no way that life could have got started, unless someone who understands the language of DNA has created it, fully complete and perfect.

Just By Chance?

Creationists are familiar with the argument that evolution is like throwing a pile of characters into the air, and they all fall down and assemble themselves into the complete text of the Encyclopaedia Britannica.

In biochemical terms, it's even worse, because there are two different versions of the same encyclopaedia, using two different character sets and a method of translating between them, The argument of chance becomes as follows:

- You throw a pile of characters (A-Z, 0-9 etc.) into the air and they all come down and form themselves into a perfect Encyclopaedia Britannica.

- You then throw a pile of binary bits (0,1) into the air and get a perfect digital Encyclopaedia Britannica which can be written to a CD-ROM.

- You then throw a pile of amorphous silicon into the air, together with a few other components, and they all come down suitably processed and assemble themselves into a computer that is capable of reading the CD-ROM and displaying the encyclopaedia on the screen.

This is the kind of absurdity that has to be contemplated, if biochemical processes are to be considered as part of evolution, and it's not surprising that evolutionists try to avoid it. They should stick with the well-known principle of biogenesis, which means that living matter can only come from living matter.

Appendix 3 - The Laws of Thermodynamics

The laws of thermodynamics are used by engineers and chemists to define the thermal processes involved in the conversion of energy into work, and the energy transfer during chemical reactions. It is a major branch of physical chemistry and is one of the most exact of all known sciences with precise mathematical definitions which have hardly changed at all since the late 19th century.

The laws of thermodynamics provide the basis on which we can build an understanding of chemical kinetics, so that chemical engineers can design process plants that operate efficiently and safely. If a chemical reaction goes too slow, the process becomes uneconomic, and if it goes too fast, it might overheat or even explode. Almost everything you touch, including the house that you live in and the clothes that you wear, have been processed in some way by the chemical industries.

I learned about the laws of thermodynamics at the Houldsworth School of Applied Science, Leeds University, where I studied chemical engineering. One day, during a lecture on physical chemistry, we were told about the implications of the Second Law of Thermodynamics. The universe is continually winding down, so that energy that is currently available for doing useful work is being redistributed so that it will eventually reach the same level everywhere and will become totally useless. Everything will become totally lifeless and all activity will cease, everywhere in the universe.

The thought crossed my mind at the time, that this was contrary to the theory of evolution, which demands that over long periods of time things get better and better. It was one of those occasions where I wondered if I should put up my hand and ask a question, but I held my peace because it would have been considered off-topic. Nobody in the chemical engineering department would have considered creation and evolution to be part of their academic discipline. Engineering is about what we can do with the earth's resources, and how to exploit them for our benefit. We don't concern ourselves

131

with how it got there, although we have to acknowledge that what we take out of the earth is unlikely to get replaced, and we have to find ways of causing minimum damage to the environment.

Although the prevailing academic philosophy was about what we can do, rather than who we are, it didn't mean we were indifferent to the question of origins. Many of us used to wonder about it during our spare time, including some of our lecturers, but it wasn't part of the engineering curriculum.

Since that time, I've heard a number of people talking about how the Second Law of Thermodynamics is incompatible with evolution, especially during recent years when creation science has been doing well, and the scientific arguments for creation have become more sophisticated.

Thermodynamics has become one of the major arguments of the creationist movement, and some biologists have been rather taken aback by it. They never studied it themselves in any great detail, although they might have touched on it briefly during a chemistry course. Now they find that creationists are using it to try and disprove evolution, and they think it's some kind of conjuring trick that we have pulled out of a hat.

Unfortunately, there are two major scientific disciplines that have gone separate ways and not had much contact with each other. On the one hand, there is applied science, which includes all the major engineering disciplines such as chemical, mechanical, electrical and civil engineering. On the other hand, there are the biological sciences, such as biology and biochemistry where evolution is considered to be foundational. Somehow, these two disciplines will have to get together and sort out their differences, although it's unlikely that engineers will give much away. They have been building steam engines, motor vehicles and chemical process plants for more than a century, based on thermodynamic principles that are known to work, while biologists have been making up theories about what might have happened to the world in the distant past, millions of years before any of them were born.

The thermodynamic debate between creationists and evolutionists often leaves much to be desired. Sometimes I hear creationists saying that entropy (the degree of disorder) always increases in a closed system, and evolutionists respond by saying that the earth isn't a closed system because it gets heated by the sun. None of them appear to understand what is meant by a closed system, and in any case, entropy tends to increase everywhere, regardless of what type of system it is. People throw word-bytes at each other, as if their next shot will undermine the other person's argument, but it soon becomes obvious that many of them have never actually studied thermodynamics.

For this reason, I have put together this appendix as a summary of the minimum information that anyone should know, before they get involved in the thermodynamics debate. Some of it is rather technical and requires a knowledge of chemistry and mathematics, but if you can persevere, the effort will be worthwhile. Anyone who can understand this appendix will not need to feel intimidated by the false claims of anti-creationists that would never be heard in any school of engineering. I have presented the laws of thermodynamics, and their implications, as simply as possible and tried to avoid lengthy mathematical derivations, but if you want to go into the subject further, there are many good books on thermodynamics and physical chemistry.[57]

Abstract

Since this is a theological book, and will be read by people of varying technical ability, I have included here a short summary of the implications of thermodynamics. There are three laws, which I have stated in the sections to follow, but we are primarily concerned with the second law which is about the random distribution of both heat and matter. In any given space where there are sources of heat in a colder environment, heat is transferred from hot bodies to cold bodies, so that eventually the whole space is at the same temperature. The same principle applies to matter, so that if a set of marbles are

---

[57] For example: Rogers & Mayhew, *Engineering Thermodynamics: Work and Heat Transfer*; Atkins, P., *The Elements of Physical Chemistry*.

arranged in the corner of a box, and the box is shaken, they will become randomly distributed around the bottom of the box. This principle affects our lives all the time, so that when people are living and working in a tidy room, it will eventually become untidy, and it gets worse and worse until you tidy it up. Disorder occurs naturally, but careful thought and planning are required to return the room to a state of order.

The Second Law of Thermodynamics also applies to physical processes, such as melting and freezing, and chemical processes that involve making and breaking chemical bonds. However, this requires that two factors are taken into account so that the overall result is a change from order to disorder. Either the process has to give off heat, which means the random distribution of heat to the environment, or else the internal structure of the substance has to become more disorderly. In some cases, both of these requirements are fulfilled, for example in the combustion of carbon.

In other cases, one condition is fulfilled and not the other. For example, when water freezes to form ice, it is transformed to a more structured and orderly state, and this is only possible because it gives off heat to the environment, so that the overall result is increased disorder.

There are some processes that will not occur by themselves, but can be made to occur by coupling them with other processes. For example, iron ore consists of a number of oxides of iron which are stable and do not break down of their own accord. However, when mixed with coke and heated in a blast furnace, they break down to produce iron because the mixture as a whole has the properties that make the reaction possible.

Taking all this together, we have the result that all processes, including the simple transfer of heat and matter, and the more complicated processes that involve physical and chemical change, occur in the direction of overall change from order to disorder. This principle applies throughout the whole universe, and it raises the question of how the universe began in an orderly state. The theological answer is that God created it that way, and there is no scientific answer, unless we accept that there is an intelligence of some sort within the universe.

The Second Law of Thermodynamics is sometimes known as the "Universal Law of Decay", and although this sounds bad, it actually produces some useful results. As heat and matter are transformed from order to disorder, some of it can be captured and used to produce useful work. One of the most important examples, as far as we are concerned, is the digestion of food.

Some Christians, who have not understood the situation correctly, have thought that the Second Law of Thermodynamics is evil and must be a consequence of the fall, but they do not realise that we cannot live without it. Even in the pre-fall days, the Second Law of Thermodynamics must have been in operation because vegetables were created as food for animals and humans, so there must have been a process of digestion. A much more reasonable suggestion is that before the fall, God sustained everything by his power, restoring things to order when it was needed. After the fall, everything began to descend relentlessly and irreversibly to disorder and will continue to do so until God creates the New Heaven and New Earth.

Thermodynamic Laws and Systems

During my engineering lectures, the three laws of thermodynamics were described as follows:

- **First Law.** Energy is neither created nor destroyed, but can be converted from one form to another.

- **Second Law.**

  (a) Heat will not flow of itself from a cold body to a hotter one.

  (b) We cannot continuously produce work by taking heat from the coldest body at our disposal.

  (c) An engine can only continuously transform heat into work by absorbing heat at a higher temperature and rejecting some of it at lower temperatures.

- **Third Law.** The entropy change between two stable states in an isothermal system becomes zero as the temperature approaches absolute zero.

For the operation of these laws, we have to define the "system" as the component we are interested in, and the "environment" as the space around it. For example if a chemical reaction is going on inside a vessel in a laboratory, we consider the vessel and its contents to be the "system" and the laboratory to be the "environment". There are a number of types of system where heat and matter might be exchanged with the environment as follows:

- **Isolated System.** There is no exchange of heat or matter, for example a process might take place in a container that is totally sealed and insulated. The universe as a whole is considered to be an isolated system because it has no environment.

- **Adiabatic System.** There is no exchange of heat, but there may be an exchange of matter. This could be represented by fluid flowing between two points in an insulated pipeline, although it is more likely to occur in engineering processes than in nature.

- **Closed System.** There is no exchange of matter, but there may be an exchange of heat, for example a process might take place in a sealed container that is not insulated against heat. The Earth is considered to be a closed system because it exchanges heat with its environment, but apart from the occasional meteorite it does not exchange matter in any significant quantity.

- **Open System.** Both heat and matter can be exchanged, for example a process might take place in an open container that is exposed to the atmosphere.

Molecular and Bulk Properties

For most practical purposes, thermodynamics is concerned with the bulk properties of matter and energy, such as heat, work, pressure, temperature, volume and mass.

On the atomic and molecular scale, changes in energy occur in discrete increments as electrons move from one energy level to another. These are known as "quantum" states, and the number of available states increases with temperature. The random distribution of energy between a wider variety of quantum states represents an increase in entropy.

There is a statistical interpretation of thermodynamics that applies to these quantum states, and it's possible to calculate the entropy of substances on this basis of this type of energy distribution, but it gets a bit complicated and we won't go into it here. Instead, we will stick to the bulk properties which are much easier to observe, and they are the manifestations of the atomic and molecular properties.

First Law of Thermodynamics

The First Law of Thermodynamics (stated on page 135) is the conservation of energy, and it takes into account all forms of energy including mechanical work. The following variables are used to describe the relationship between heat and work:

U The internal energy of the system. This is the sum of the potential and kinetic energies associated with the random motion of atoms, molecules and ions in the system. It is not possible to measure an absolute value, but changes in the internal energy (ΔU) are used to keep an inventory of any transfers of energy passing into or out of the system.

Q The heat input to the system from the environment.

W The work done by the system on the environment. For example, the expansion of a gas might be used to push a piston, and the work is defined as the force multiplied by the distance.

The balance between heat and work is defined as follows:

$$\Delta U = Q - W \qquad (1)$$

This represents a generalised system where both the pressure (P) and the volume (V) might change, and the work done by expansion into the environment is:

$$W = \Delta(PV) \qquad (2)$$

If the system is in a closed container so that the volume is held constant, there is no opportunity to do work on the environment. The internal energy change at constant volume (V) is:

$$\Delta U_V = Q \qquad\qquad (3)$$

If the system is a gas that is freely allowed to expand, the internal energy at constant pressure (P) is:

$$\Delta U_p = Q - P\Delta V \qquad\qquad (4)$$

Note: Sometimes W is defined as the work done on the system by the environment, in which case we have ($\Delta U = Q + W$), but we also have ($W = -P\Delta V$) so the result is the same.

To accommodate the wide variety of processes occurring at atmospheric pressure, possibly with gases being given off and expanding, we define the enthalpy (H) to represent the total energy, including the internal energy and the work component associated with the pressure and volume of the gas.

$$H = U + PV \qquad\qquad (5)$$

At constant pressure we have:

$$\Delta H = \Delta U_p + P\Delta V \qquad\qquad (6)$$

If we re-write equation (4) so that the heat input Q is on the left we have:

$$Q = \Delta U_p + P\Delta V \qquad\qquad (7)$$

Comparing this with equation (6)we have:

$$\Delta H = Q \qquad\qquad (8)$$

This is an important result because it means the enthalpy change is directly equal to the heat input. We cannot measure enthalpy directly, but we can calculate changes in enthalpy, based on the heat added to the system, or the heat given off to the environment. Standard values are defined for calculation purposes, on the basis that elements in their normal state (solid, liquid or gas) at 25°C (298.15°K) have a datum value of H=0.

Second Law of Thermodynamics

The Second Law of Thermodynamics (stated on page 135) describes the direction of flow of heat and the conditions under which it can be transformed into work. It always flows from a hot body to a colder one, so that heat which is concentrated in one place becomes randomly distributed to its environment. In the process of distribution, it is capable of doing useful work, but never with 100% efficiency. For example, work is done by the transfer of heat to a steam engine, but you lose some of the heat with the combustion gases and waste steam that go up the chimney.

The dispersal of heat to the environment represents a change from order to disorder. It happens continuously throughout the whole universe, and this is why the Second Law of Thermodynamics is sometimes called the Universal Law of Decay. The heat given off by the stars is dispersed into space until everything is at the same temperature and there is no further opportunity for conversion of heat into work. At that point the universe will be totally lifeless and all physical and chemical processes will cease.

While there is still life in the universe, and particularly in our solar system, the Earth will continue to operate like a rotating machine. It receives heat from the Sun and gives it off into space, and in the process some work is done. One side of the Earth heats up while the other cools down, and there is a cycle of heating and cooling as the Earth rotates. This causes pressure changes in the atmosphere, so that the wind blows, and water from the oceans is picked up and deposited on the continents. The energy received by the Earth follows the Second Law, so that it becomes dispersed and disordered.

The process of dispersion continues at the local level, as any given point on the Earth, exposed to its environment, tends to disperse its energy in the usual way, although it can be temporarily raised to a higher energy state by interaction with its environment under certain specialised conditions, for example by close proximity with something that is in a state of combustion.

There are a number of ways of expressing the Second Law of Thermodynamics and it appears slightly different in every textbook. The version on page 135 is the "power thermodynamics" version which describes the conversion of heat into mechanical work. However, soon after these laws had been written on the blackboard at the engineering school, lots of chemical equations began to appear. The reason is that the laws of thermodynamics are not limited to heat and mechanical work. They describe the distribution of energy in a much more general sense, including the energy that is transferred between substances during chemical reactions.

Entropy

The degree of thermal disorder, as energy disperses to its environment, is called *entropy*. The differential change in entropy, as a consequence of heat transfer at a given absolute temperature (T) is:

$$dS = dQ / T \tag{9}$$

This can be derived mathematically, on the basis that thermal disorder represents the capacity for change and it has to be a function of the heat content. However, it involves the solution of perfect (or exact) differential equations and we won't get into that here because it's a bit too complicated, but it's easy enough to appreciate why temperature should appear on the bottom line of the equation. Temperature determines the significance of an energy change, so that the change has more significance at low temperature than at high temperature. It might be considered the thermal equivalent of noise. For example, if you are in a quiet library and you make a loud noise, everybody will look around in astonishment, but if you are at a football match nobody will notice.

For a system at constant volume, the heat transfer can be calculated from the heat capacity (C_V), so we have:

$$dS = (C_V / T) \, dT \qquad (10)$$

For a system at constant pressure, we use the heat capacity (C_p), so we have:

$$dS = (C_p / T) \, dT \qquad (11)$$

It is possible to calculate the absolute value of the entropy (S) from the Third Law of Thermodynamics, and we will get to that question soon, but for most purposes we are only concerned with the change of entropy (ΔS). We have already seen, from equation (8), that under conditions of constant pressure, the enthalpy change (ΔH) represents the heat input to the system from the environment, so the negative value ($-\Delta H$) represents the heat given off to the environment. In that case, the entropy change of the environment is:

$$\Delta S_{ENV} = -\Delta H / T \qquad (12)$$

This is an important result which will be used later in the discussion of chemical reactions.

Third Law of Thermodynamics

We have already seen, from the statement of the Third Law of Thermodynamics on page 135, that the entropy change between stable states becomes zero as the temperature approaches absolute zero. This enables us to set a datum value (S=0) for all substances at absolute zero of temperature. It requires that we use an absolute scale of temperature for all thermodynamic processes, so we use the Kelvin scale where $0°K = -273.15°C$.

To calculate the absolute value of entropy (S), you have to integrate equation (10) or (11) as appropriate, all the way up from absolute zero to the working temperature, but for engineering purposes, tabulated lists and charts of standard entropy values are available for various substances, sometimes comparing the values with other thermodynamic data.

Distribution of Energy

The distribution of energy, from a local system to its environment, is always accompanied by an overall increase in entropy. To explain why this should happen, consider a kettle of water that is boiling in your kitchen. If you turn off the gas, the kettle will cool down, and as it does so the kitchen will warm up, until eventually they are both at the same temperature and are in a state of equilibrium. During the transfer, the heat lost by the kettle is the same as the heat gained by the kitchen, but the changes in entropy are different because they represent the heat change divided by the temperature (dQ/T). The kitchen is at a lower temperature than the kettle during the transfer, so the entropy gained by the kitchen is greater than the entropy lost by the kettle. There is an overall gain in entropy, as a consequence of the distribution of heat.

The same principle works in reverse. If you place a glass of cold water in a warm room, it will warm up and will cool the room slightly. The water will gain more entropy than is lost by the room so there is an overall increase in entropy.

It doesn't matter how you look at it, as heat is dispersed and things move to a state of equilibrium, there is always an increase in entropy. Sometimes people ask "How can you say that entropy always increases? What about the freezing of water?" The answer is the same. If you place a glass of water in an environment that is below freezing point, the water will freeze and will lose entropy, but will give up its latent heat to the environment causing an overall increase in entropy. Then if you melt the ice you will again have an increase in entropy. But you might ask another question: "If you freeze water and then melt the ice, don't you return to the same conditions?" The answer is no, because you need two different environments, the refrigerator where the water freezes, and the room where the ice melts. You have to generate electricity to run the refrigerator, and this requires a power station which burns fuel and contributes entropy to the environment.

Conditions for Spontaneous Change

In an isolated system, for example the universe as a whole, the direction of thermodynamic processes are defined as follows:

- Natural (spontaneous) processes take place in a direction such that entropy tends to increase ($\Delta S > 0$).

- Unnatural processes do not take place spontaneously because they would cause the entropy to decrease ($\Delta S < 0$). They have to be driven by other processes so that the overall result is an increase in entropy.

- Reversible processes are the limits of natural processes, where entropy does not change ($\Delta S = 0$).

In a system that is not isolated, we have to consider both the system and environment, as already explained, and we have seen a number of examples of natural processes where things warm up or cool down until they reach equilibrium with their environment.

An example of an unnatural process would be a kettle of water that heats up, extracting heat from a cold room with the gas turned off. Clearly this is an impossible situation, and it is represented in thermodynamic terms by an overall decrease in entropy. We all know that to heat up a kettle of water, you have to turn on the gas, so we come back to the real world where entropy increases.

There are no truly reversible thermodynamic processes, but it is possible to approach reversibility when the temperature change is very small. For example, if you have a block of ice at freezing point, in a room that is just above freezing point, the ice will melt very slowly. and there will be a small increase in the overall entropy. Conversely, if you have a glass of water at freezing point, in a room that is just below freezing point, the water will freeze very slowly and there will be a small increase in the overall entropy. In both cases, entropy increases, but if the temperature difference between the system and environment is infinitely small, the process will take an infinitely long time, and the entropy increase will approach zero.

Conversion of Heat into Work

Now we will look at the application of thermodynamics to engine design, known as *power thermodynamics*. The transfer of heat can be accompanied by the conversion of heat into useful work, but never with 100% efficiency. Some of the heat has to be discarded to the environment. For example, when you drive your car, the heat generated by the fuel is used to create work, but some of the heat is discarded, mainly through the exhaust pipe. The internal combustion engine is a specific example of a heat engine where thermodynamic values have to be calculated for each part of the cycle, but all heat engines conform to the same generalised description, that a quantity of heat (Q_H) is taken from a hot source and a smaller quantity (Q_C) is discarded to a cold sink. The conversion of heat into work is represented by the First Law of Thermodynamics, and under steady state conditions where there is no overall change in the internal energy of the system ($\Delta U = 0$), the work done is:

$$W = Q_H - Q_C \qquad (13)$$

The efficiency is:

$$\eta = (W/Q_H) = (Q_H - Q_C) / Q_H \qquad (14)$$

The question is, how can you minimise the amount of heat discarded and get the maximum amount of work? The Second Law of Thermodynamics demands that the overall entropy of the system and the environment has to increase, so the heat discarded has to be enough to meet this requirement. This places a limit on the theoretical maximum amount of work that can be obtained, which has to be less than the heat input Q_H. To achieve this theoretical maximum, the process has to be reversible, operating at the limits of a natural process where the entropy change approaches zero. This can only be achieved in practice by running the engine infinitely slowly, so we have a situation that is similar to the freezing of water and melting of ice, already mentioned, which also has to be done infinitely slowly to achieve a zero increase of entropy.

In 1824, Sadi Carnot defined an idealised engine cycle which would achieve the theoretical maximum efficiency. This is known as the *Carnot cycle*, consisting of a cylinder with a piston that moves in response to the expansion and compression of a gas. The pressure-volume (P-V) diagram is as follows:

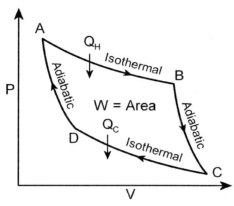

Figure 3.1 - Carnot Cycle

There are four stages in the cycle:

A → B   Isothermal expansion. The gas expands in contact with a source of heat, but without any change in temperature.

B → C   Adiabatic expansion. The gas is cut off from the source of heat, but continues to expand, causing the temperature to fall.

C → D   Isothermal compression. The gas is compressed, in contact with a heat sink, but without any change in temperature.

D → A   Adiabatic compression. The gas is cut off from the heat sink, but continues to be compressed, causing the temperature to rise.

The work done by this cycle is represented by the area enclosed within the curve, and by considering the properties of each part of the cycle, it can be shown that the efficiency depends on the absolute temperature of the hot source (T_H) and the cold sink (T_C) as follows:

$$\eta = (T_H - T_C)/T_H \qquad (15)$$

The derivation of this equation is available from any good textbook on engineering thermodynamics.[58]

The efficiency of the Carnot cycle can only reach 100% when heat is discarded at absolute zero of temperature, a condition that can never be achieved in practice. This means that even in the idealised conditions of the Carnot cycle, the theoretical maximum efficiency is always less than 100%. For all practical purposes, we have to operate at less than the theoretical maximum, because a perfect Carnot cycle is impossible to perform. The two isothermal stages take an infinitely long time because they require that heat is transferred across an infinitesimally small temperature difference. This means that although the efficiency is maximised, the performance approaches zero.

Clearly, this is an undesirable situation for a practical engine, and to achieve any realistic performance, it has to operate at substantially less than the theoretical maximum efficiency. It's possible for motor vehicles to travel long distances on small amounts of fuel, but to achieve it you have to drive slowly, and it might not be what you want. As soon as you put your foot on the accelerator, the performance increases, but the efficiency decreases because large amounts of heat are being discharged through the exhaust. The heat input to the engine still has to satisfy the requirement for conversion of heat into work, so more fuel is consumed. At high levels of performance, for example in racing cars, the fuel consumed becomes totally disproportionate to the distance travelled.

Engineers have to take into account the balance between performance and efficiency when designing engines for any particular purpose, and to achieve the best results, they try to maintain a high temperature difference between the source and sink.

---

[58] For example: Rogers & Mayhew, *Engineering Thermodynamics: Work and Heat Transfer.*

Exergy

We have seen that, as heat is transferred from a high temperature to a low temperature, some of it can be converted to useful work, but not all of it, because of the requirement to discard heat at low temperature. The amount of energy that is available for conversion to work is called *exergy*, although it is sometimes called *availability*.

As energy becomes distributed around the universe, the total quantity of energy remains the same, but less and less of it is available for conversion to work, so there is a continuous destruction of exergy. Eventually, exergy will approach zero and no work will be possible. The distribution of energy means that entropy increases while exergy decreases, but these are just two different ways of saying the same thing, that eventually the universe will be totally lifeless. It means that in the beginning, there must have been low entropy and high exergy, before the universe began its gradual slide to oblivion.

Thermodynamics of Chemical Processes

Now we move on to processes that are more complex than the heating and cooling of water, or the conversion of heat into work. We will consider the circumstances in which molecules of a substance will break up and recombine into different substances.

The principles are basically the same as for the processes considered already, except that you have to account for the entropies of all the reactants and products, together with the entropy of the environment, and if there is an overall increase in entropy, the reaction is thermodynamically possible.

For example, when iron rusts, you have to take into account the entropy of the reactants (iron and oxygen), the entropy of the product (iron oxide) and the entropy change of the atmosphere that has gained heat from the reaction. We all know that iron rusts spontaneously, and it causes our cars to fall apart. The reason why it happens is because the total entropy change is positive.

To calculate the conditions under which a reaction will proceed, we have to consider the total entropy of the system and environment in terms of the system alone which is easier to measure, and find a way to eliminate the environment from the calculation. For this purpose we have the following variables:

ΔS The entropy change of the system, including all the reactants and products.

ΔS_{ENV} The entropy change of the environment.

ΔS_{TOTAL} The total entropy change of the system and environment.

These are related as follows:

$$\Delta S_{TOTAL} = \Delta S + \Delta S_{ENV} \tag{16}$$

However, for a system at constant pressure, the entropy change of the environment is given in equation (12), so we can eliminate it by substitution, leaving us with:

$$\Delta S_{TOTAL} = \Delta S - \Delta H/T \tag{17}$$

Multiplying by -T we have:

$$-T\Delta S_{TOTAL} = \Delta H - T\Delta S \tag{18}$$

This enables us to define the Gibbs free energy:

$$G = H - TS \tag{19}$$

The change in Gibbs free energy at constant temperature and pressure is:

$$\Delta G = \Delta H - T\Delta S \tag{20}$$

Comparing this with equation (18) we have the result that a reduction in the Gibbs free energy corresponds to an increase in the total entropy, therefore it defines a spontaneous reaction. This means the conditions for spontaneity are as follows:

($\Delta G < 0$)   Spontaneous process. Reactants are converted into products.

($\Delta G > 0$)   Non-spontaneous process. If products have been formed already, as a consequence of other processes, they will be converted back to reactants.

($\Delta G = 0$)   This represents the limit of spontaneity where the reactants and products have the same value of G.

The Gibbs free energy represents the energy available to perform a chemical reaction, and is the chemical equivalent of exergy. If a reaction is spontaneous, it is known as *exergonic*. If it is non-spontaneous, it is *endergonic*.

In a reaction mixture, containing both reactants and products, the value of G does not vary uniformly as the reaction proceeds. Instead, it descends to a level that is lower than both the pure reactants and products, so there is an equilibrium point where the reaction does not go in either direction.

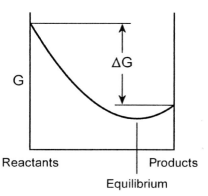

Figure 3.2 - Equilibrium point in a reaction mixture

Figure 3.2 shows a reaction where the overall ΔG is negative, and the reaction proceeds to the minimum value at the equilibrium point. If the curve was inverted as a mirror image, so that G was higher on the right than on the left, it would still have a minimum value between the two of them, and it would be possible to get some products as the mixture goes to equilibrium.

The equilibrium point is defined by the equilibrium constant K which represents the relative proportions of reactants and products, and for this purpose we use the *activities* of the components which can be thought of as an effective concentration which has been modified as a consequence of the behaviour of the substance in a mixture. We won't get into all the details here about how the activity might differ from the concentration, but we have the following simplified cases:

- For gases at atmospheric pressure, the activity is the partial pressure.
- For solutes the activity is the molar concentration.
- For pure solids and liquids the activity is 1.

Consider an example where reactants are converted to products in the following stoichiometric proportions:

$$2A + B \rightarrow 3C + D \tag{21}$$

If a, b, c, d represent the activities of the components A, B, C, D at equilibrium, we have:

$$K = c^3 d / a^2 b \tag{22}$$

The equilibrium constant can also be related to the overall change of Gibbs free energy, the gas constant R and the absolute temperature T as follows:

$$K = e^{-(\Delta G/RT)} \tag{23}$$

The derivation of this equation can be found in any good textbook on physical chemistry,[59] but it can be seen that K has the following properties:

---

[59] For example: Atkins, P., *The Elements of Physical Chemistry.*

- For a spontaneous process ($\Delta G < 0$), K > 1.

- For a non-spontaneous process ($\Delta G > 0$), K < 1.

- For a process at the limits of spontaneity ($\Delta G = 0$), K = 1.

The value of K represents how far the reaction will proceed to completion, so that a large value of K means the reactants will be almost completely converted into products.

The rate of the reaction depends on the relative proportions of reactants and products, so that it slows down as it reaches equilibrium. It also depends on temperature and is restrained by a quantity called the activation energy, as we will soon see.

For the purpose of calculating the value of ΔG from equation (20), standard values of enthalpy are available for a wide range of substances, in terms of the heats of formation of compounds from their elements, together with standard values of entropy. Lists of tabulated data can be found in any good textbook on physical chemistry, and it is possible to calculate ΔG for many reactions. Sometimes the Gibbs free energy of formation of compounds from their elements is included in the tabulated lists.

The term (G = H - TS) can be understood as an inventory of stored energy. The enthalpy (H) is the energy that can be given off as heat. The term (TS) is the energy associated with the random, disorderly motion of molecules. In that case, G represents the energy that is stored in an orderly way, in the arrangement and motion of the molecules. This energy is available for doing work, which is an orderly process, but it excludes any work that might be done by the expansion of the system. It is known as *non-expansion work* because it occurs within the substance itself and is available for a variety of purposes, including the arrangement of bonds in chemical reactions where new molecules are formed. This is why it is called *Gibbs free energy*. It is available to perform processes within the system without the burden of having to contribute something to the environment. It is named after J.W. Gibbs (1839-1903), the American professor of mathematical physics at Yale College, New Haven, who established the principles of chemical thermodynamics.

Temperature Dependence of Spontaneity

It is clear from the equation ($\Delta G = \Delta H - T\Delta S$) that if the spontaneity of a reaction depends on ΔG being negative, then in some circumstances it will depend on temperature as follows:

- If ΔH is negative and ΔS is positive, the reaction will be possible at all temperatures.

- If ΔH is positive and ΔS is negative, the reaction will not be possible at any temperature.

- If ΔH is positive and ΔS is positive, the reaction will be possible at a high temperature ($T > \Delta H/\Delta S$)

- If ΔH is negative and ΔS is negative, the reaction will be possible at a low temperature ($T < \Delta H/\Delta S$)

The situation is illustrated in the following diagram:

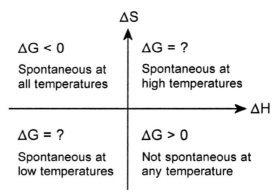

Figure 3.3 - Temperature dependence of spontaneity

Activation Energy

If the Gibbs free energy was the only criterion that determines the progress of a chemical reaction, we would be in big trouble. Consider, for example, the combustion of carbon.

$$C + O_2 \rightarrow CO_2 \qquad (24)$$

The thermodynamic variables for this reaction are:

$\Delta H = -393.51$ kJ/mol

$\Delta S = +2.862$ J/mol°K

$\Delta G = \Delta H - T\Delta S$
    $= -394.36$ kJ/mol at 298.15°K

Note: In all calculations involving ΔH and ΔS you have to divide ΔS by 1000 because it uses joules, not kilojoules.

This reaction has a large negative enthalpy change and a small positive entropy change. There is a loss of Gibbs free energy so the reaction is always spontaneous. In that case, if the reaction depended entirely on ΔG, many carbon-based materials would immediately burst into flames. There would be complete chaos all around us and all life would be impossible.

Fortunately, most chemical reactions are restrained by the requirement for an additional amount of energy called the activation energy, and this is the reason why we say that a reaction *tends* to proceed if there is a loss of Gibbs free energy. We know in practice that many reactions don't start straight away, and they need a push to get them started. For example, a candle will not burn until you light it with a match, but once ignited, it will continue to burn until all the wax has gone. The same applies to many flammable substances, and we have to avoid lighting things that will burn catastrophically. If you drop a match onto flammable furniture, a small area will begin to burn, and this will have enough energy to ignite a larger area around it, and the fire will spread until all the furniture and all other combustible material in the house is going up in flames.

The Swedish chemist, Svante Arrhenius (1859 - 1927) investigated an increasing amount of published data on reaction rates, and discovered that in the vast majority of cases, the reaction rate (k) varies logarithmically with the inverse of temperature as follows:

$$\ln k \propto (1 / T) \qquad (25)$$

He found that the data could be plotted graphically giving a straight line with a negative slope as follows:

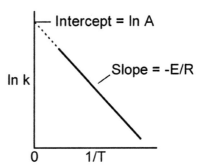

Figure 3.4 - Temperature dependence of reaction rate

This enabled him to define constants which could be fitted to the following equation:

$$\ln k = \ln A - (E/RT) \tag{26}$$

Or alternatively:

$$k = Ae^{-E/RT} \tag{27}$$

The constants are:

A   The pre-exponential factor which gives the maximum reaction rate at high temperature where (E/RT) approaches zero. Clearly this is just a theoretical maximum because the reactants would disintegrate as the temperature approaches infinity. The value is obtained from the graph by extrapolating towards the vertical axis.

E   The activation energy which defines the temperature dependence of the reaction rate. The value is obtained from the slope of the graph. The higher the value, the more the reaction will depend on temperature.

The activation energy has the effect of slowing down a chemical reaction, and if it is high enough, it might slow down the reaction so much that it becomes hardly perceptible. Then if the temperature is raised, the term (E/RT) is reduced and the reaction proceeds at an observable rate.

Although a reaction might be feasible, in terms of a loss of Gibbs free energy, the activation energy (E) represents an obstruction to the reaction as follows:

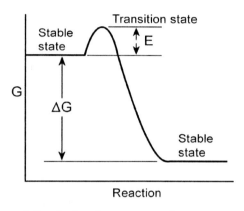

Figure 3.5 - Activation energy obstructs reaction

The reactants are initially in a stable state at a high energy level, and the reaction is held back by the requirement for the activation energy. When this additional amount of energy is added, the reactants are raised to the transition state and the reaction proceeds, until it reaches a new stable state at a lower energy level corresponding to the reaction products. The difference between the initial and final states is the Gibbs free energy ($\Delta G < 0$).

The activation energy presents a barrier to the reaction, but it does not obstruct the reaction entirely. Instead, it controls the rate, and it is easy enough to see why this works at the molecular level. Some molecules will react and others will not, depending on their energy states which are distributed around an average. The molecules with enough energy to overcome the activation barrier and reach the transition state will react, and the lower energy molecules will not.

It is possible to show, from probability theory, that in a distribution of molecular energy levels, the number of molecules exceeding a given energy level follows the same profile as equation (27), so this can be directly related to the reaction rate (k). The energy levels follow the Maxwell-Boltzmann distribution as follows:

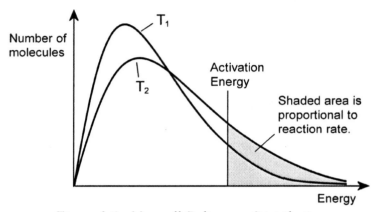

Figure 3.6 - Maxwell-Boltzmann Distribution

The shaded area on the right represents the molecules that have exceeded the activation energy. There are two curves for different temperatures $(T_2 > T_1)$ and a larger proportion of molecules exceed the activation energy at the higher temperature, giving a faster reaction rate. If the activation energy for a reaction is high, the shaded area will occupy just a small region at the right, so that only a small proportion of the molecules will achieve the transition state and the reaction will go slowly.

The distribution of energy levels among the molecules is such that there is no upper limit, and a small number of molecules might reach the transition state even when the activation energy is high and the temperature is low. In that case, as long the reaction is thermodynamically possible (defined by $\Delta G < 0$), it will always proceed, even though it might be very slow.

When you take some charcoal to light a barbecue, it is actually burning before you set fire to it. You wouldn't notice anything when handling just a few small lumps of charcoal, but slow burning is detectable in large volumes of carbon such as in coal mines, especially where there is coal dust which has a larger surface area per unit volume and is more reactive.

Coupling of Non-Spontaneous Processes

It is possible for a chemical reaction to proceed in the direction of increasing Gibbs free energy, but only if the reaction is coupled with one or more other reactions, such that the combined Gibbs free energy is decreased and the total entropy of the system and environment is increased. Figure 3.7 shows how a spontaneous reaction can be used to drive a non-spontaneous reaction.

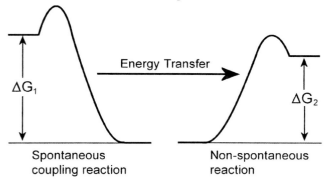

Figure 3.7 - Reaction coupling

An example is the production of iron in a blast furnace. The objective is to achieve the following separation of iron from iron oxide:

$$2Fe_2O_3 \rightarrow 4Fe + 3O_2 \qquad (28)$$

The thermodynamic variables for this reaction are:

$\Delta H = +1648.4$ kJ/mol

$\Delta S = +549.73$ J/mol°K

$\Delta G = \Delta H - T\Delta S$
$\quad\quad = +1484.49$ kJ/mol at 298.15°K

This reaction has positive ΔH and ΔS, and assuming that these remain reasonably constant over a temperature range, we can calculate the temperature at which the reaction becomes thermodynamically possible:

$$
\begin{aligned}
T &= \Delta H / \Delta S \\
&= 1648.4 / 0.54973 \\
&= 2998.5°K
\end{aligned}
$$

This colossal temperature could not be achieved in any practical processes. Instead we set up a coupling reaction by burning coke:

$$3C + 3O_2 \rightarrow 3CO_2 \tag{29}$$

We already have the thermodynamic variables for this reaction, from equation (24) and we multiply by three to obtain:

$\Delta G = -1183.08$ kJ/mol at 298.15°K

This is a large negative ΔG, but still not enough for the coupling process. Combining equations (28) and (29) we have the following coupled reaction:

$$2Fe_2O_3 + 3C \rightarrow 4Fe + 3CO_2 \tag{30}$$

For this, we have the following thermodynamic variables:

$\Delta H = +467.87$ kJ/mol

$\Delta S = +558.32$ J/mol°K

$\Delta G = +301.41$ kJ/mol at 298.15°K

We still have positive ΔG at ambient temperature, but we are working at a much higher temperature because we are burning coke. The temperature at which the reaction becomes thermodynamically possible is:

$$T = \Delta H / \Delta S$$
$$= 467.87 / 0.55832$$
$$= 838.00°K$$
$$= 564.85°C$$

In practice, the reaction is a bit more complicated and goes through a number of intermediate stages, and in the smelting process there is a temperature variation from about 200°C at the top of the furnace where the gases emerge, to about 2000°C at the bottom where the coke is burnt and the molten iron is separated from its impurities.

The smelting process requires that iron ore is reduced to iron under carefully controlled conditions. The ore is mixed with coke and fed into the top of the furnace where it slowly descends through the rising column of hot gases. Hot air is fed into the bottom of the furnace, where the coke burns, giving off carbon dioxide (CO_2). This reacts with unburnt coke, further up the furnace, producing carbon monoxide (CO). The overall reaction, up to this point, is:

$$2C + O_2 \rightarrow 2CO \qquad (31)$$

There are various types of iron ore containing different oxides of iron. The hot carbon monoxide reacts with the oxides, reducing them in stages as follows:

$$3Fe_2O_3 + CO \rightarrow 2Fe_3O_4 + CO_2 \qquad (32)$$

$$Fe_3O_4 + CO \rightarrow 3FeO + CO_2 \qquad (33)$$

$$FeO + CO \rightarrow Fe + CO_2 \qquad (34)$$

Limestone ($CaCO_3$) is added to the furnace as a flux, to remove siliceous impurities and sulphur, creating a mixture called "slag". The iron and slag drain down to the bottom of the furnace, where they separate out with the slag floating on the molten iron, and they can be drained off separately.

This process requires enormous amounts of heat, causing a large increase in the entropy of the system and its environment. Large amounts of heat are discharged with the hot gases from the top of the furnace, and with the molten iron and slag that have to be removed from the bottom.

The resulting iron has a higher Gibbs free energy than the ore from which it was extracted, according to the thermodynamics of equation (28). This has been achieved by coupling it with another process that goes to a lower energy state. Coupling is one of the most important principles of chemical thermodynamics. When chemists are looking for ways to perform non-spontaneous processes, they try to find spontaneous processes with which they might be coupled.

Falling Back Down Again

The products of a non-spontaneous process are inherently less stable than the reactants from which they were formed, because energy has become concentrated in the products and will tend to disperse if a suitable path exists for a reverse reaction.

After all the effort that has been made to produce iron, and all the expenditure of energy, we know that it could all come to nothing. A reverse reaction occurs as soon as the iron is exposed to atmospheric oxygen and water. This is a simple electrochemical process where iron is oxidised in one region of the surface and dissolved oxygen is reduced in another.

It is also possible for iron to oxidise by combustion, but it does not happen easily because it requires a high activation energy. Steel wool can be made to burn in air, using a candle or a match, because it has a high surface area compared with the volume. Thicker slabs of iron can be made to burn in pure oxygen at a high temperature, and this method is used for flamecutting.

If a natural reaction is possible, it is most likely to go by the simplest possible route. Some organisation is required to achieve combustion of iron, but rusting occurs without any intervention, and we have to paint our cars to prevent it from happening.

Molecules of Life

It is sometimes argued that the laws of thermodynamics do not present any real obstruction to the formation of complex, high-energy molecules, such as those that are found in biological life, because given enough time, the right components will come together by chance, and heat from the Sun will supply the required energy. However, this would be missing the point, that if you have to rely on time and chance, it is much more likely that natural processes will occur than unnatural ones.

We have seen how iron has to be produced with meticulous care, and then the process goes into reverse, so that the iron turns to rust as soon as it is given a suitable opportunity. The same is true of other high-energy substances, because the path downhill is easier than the path uphill. If a few million years are needed to produce a high-energy molecule, it is likely that it will disintegrate into its low-energy components in a lot less time.

To create complex molecules, you might on some occasions be fortunate enough to do it using natural processes, but on other occasions you will have to use unnatural processes. It all depends on what you want to produce. If you want to produce the complex molecules of life (which is impossible anyway for reasons I have explained in Appendix 2), you will have to create many complex molecules in high energy states, using unnatural processes. This will require a long sequence of unnatural reactions, each requiring its own coupling process to drive the energy level upwards. It's rather like climbing a mountain using a series of interconnecting paths, but it isn't a straightforward sequence from the bottom to the top. It's more like a number of climbers all starting at different points around the mountain, climbing different paths and occasionally meeting each other in small groups along the way. It's not an easy journey, because each path represents an unnatural process that requires coupling with one or more natural processes. If everything happens by chance, as suggested by evolution, it means that each climber has to wait at the bottom of the path until someone comes along who can give him a push. He cannot ask for help from other climbers, but he can look out for other people who might be passing by. Most of the people who pass by will be unable to help, but eventually a very special person might come, who is associated with that particular path, and gives him the required push. Then the climber waits at the bottom of another path, waiting for another very special person to pass by, and he gets another push. All these special people have to arrive at the right time, so that he meets the other climbers at the appropriate points up the mountain, and eventually they all arrive at the top.

Clearly, this is an impossible situation, and complex molecules would not be able to form under these conditions. If a few of them managed to get part of the way, they would come tumbling down again because natural processes occur much more easily.

We have seen in Appendix 2 that chemical evolution is impossible because meaningful information has to exist in two different character sets, with a method of translating between them, and now we find that the molecules cannot evolve for thermodynamic reasons, giving an even greater level of impossibility.

General Disorder

The Second Law of Thermodynamics has consequences that go beyond the actual transfer of energy and change of chemical state. It creates chaos and disorder everywhere, so that cars wear out and buildings fall down. However, there are no thermodynamic equations that will distinguish between a new car in a showroom and an old one falling to bits on a scrap heap. The thermodynamic considerations are limited to the thermal and chemical changes that have occurred.

For example, if a car falls apart because it has rusted, it is possible to calculate the entropy change associated with the rusting of iron. If a building falls down because the materials have deteriorated, the entropy change can also be calculated.

The actual consequences of a thermodynamic process are dependent on our perceptions. A car is made of iron and other materials, and it fulfils its purpose as long as all the materials remain in their original state, but if some of them change into something else, the car will be useless. Of course, some people might have a different view of what they consider to be useful. I once went to an art gallery where an old car battery and a hand-operated air pump were placed together on the floor as an exhibit. Some people might consider a new car to be ugly, and a rusty old banger to be a work of art, and for them, the Second Law of Thermodynamics does not create disorder. However, if they create something for themselves that suits their own purposes, and leave it exposed to the ravages of chemistry, it will change into something else, so it will represent chaos and disorder.

Sometimes, things happen that are only an indirect result of thermodynamics. Buildings fall down, not because of chemical changes in the materials, but because of mechanical battering from the weather. There is no way of measuring entropy in terms of the distribution of bricks on the ground, but we know that the weather is a thermodynamic process, driven by heat from the Sun, and therefore the destruction of a building can be indirectly related to the thermodynamics of the atmosphere.

However you look at it, there is no intelligence associated with the Second Law of Thermodynamics. It is capable of doing things that are useful for the existence of life, for example depositing rain on the earth, but only because life is there and is capable of making use of the rain. Otherwise, it causes destruction wherever it goes, including sometimes depositing too much rain, and it is oblivious to the consequences. Everything is scattered at random, not just in terms of energy distribution, but in the distribution of everything.

Appendix 4 - Cosmology

The Earth is the third planet from the Sun, in a solar system that contains nine observable planets. The Sun is a star within a galaxy called the Milky Way, made up of 100 billion stars. There are more than 10 billion galaxies in the universe, separated by vast distances.

The Milky Way is a typical spiral galaxy, shaped like a disk with spiral arms and a bulge at the centre. Our Sun has no special position in the galaxy. It is neither at the centre nor at the edge, but part of the way out on one of the spiral arms.

If you go out on a clear night, to a place that is relatively free of light pollution from nearby buildings and street lamps you can see a faint, broad band of light stretching from one horizon to the other. You can vaguely make out that it's made up of very large numbers of tiny dots. These are just some of the distant stars of the Milky Way.

If you look into space with a telescope, you might be able see other galaxies, each as big as our own, but because they are so far away they look like tiny dots in the sky. If your telescope is powerful enough you might be able to see the shape of the spiral arms of some of the nearest galaxies. Astronomers have estimated that the most distant galaxies in the visible universe are about 15 billion light years away.

The edge of the visible universe is known as the *horizon*. It represents the longest distance that we can see into space, because of the time required for light to travel from that region. We cannot see anything beyond the horizon because, if anything exists there, the light has not reached us yet since the universe was formed.

Since the horizon is about 15 billion light years away, it follows that the universe must be 15 billion years old. In that case, how do we reconcile modern astronomy with the six days of creation described in Genesis, and the formation of the Sun, Moon and stars on the fourth day? Some people would say that each of these "days" represents a long period of millions or even billions of years, but the Bible does not allow that possibility. The Hebrew word *yom*, when used for counting days as it does in Genesis, means ordinary days of

24 hours. Each day is described as an evening and a morning, so there can be no ambiguity, and the days of Creation are subsequently used in the Ten Commandments to define the six working days followed by the Sabbath. (Exodus 20:8-11). Also, what are we to make of the remainder of Biblical history which estimates about 6000 years for the age of the Earth since Creation, based on the ages of successive patriarchs and kings?

Have the astronomers got their measurements wrong, or is there something wrong with our interpretation of the Bible? Alternatively, is there something about the universe and its physical laws that we have not understood?

Measurement of the Universe

There are various methods of measuring distances in space. The method for measuring relatively short distances, within our own solar system and to the nearest stars, is by triangulation. The principle is that if you move sideways while you are looking at something, you will see it from a different angle, and the change in the angle enables you to calculate the distance.

To measure the distance from the Earth to the Sun, two astronomers on opposite sides of the Earth have to make simultaneous measurements of the position of the Sun.

To measure the distance to a nearby star, the diameter of the Earth does not give a large enough base line for the measurement. Instead, you have to use the movement of the Earth as it travels from one side of the Sun to the other every six months. The nearby stars will appear displaced against the background of distant stars, so the angle of displacement enables you to calculate the distance.

The measurement of the distance to remote stars is more complicated, and it is estimated from their size, luminosity and red shift. There are ways of criticising the methods, and they might not be totally accurate, but there is no way to get down from billions of light years to the 6,000 years that are suggested by Biblical creation.

Light in Transit

Some creationists have suggested that God created the stars at great distances away from us in space, and at the same time created the light that is coming from them. However, this does not have much support because light carries information about events that are supposed to have happened in the past, for example the birth and death of stars.

When we observe something happening a million light years away, we are led to believe that it occurred a million years ago, but if the universe is only 6000 years old, it means the event never happened. The light that reaches us from space would be misleading, and it is difficult to believe that God would deceive us by creating light in that way.

Decrease in the Speed of Light

The speed of light in a vacuum is normally thought to be constant, at a rate of 186,000 miles/second. However, there is reason to believe that the speed of light is slowing down, and this theory, supported by some observations, is known as CDK (c-decay). Various other physical constants are related to the speed of light, for example charge to mass ratio, permeability and Planck's constant (the smallest amount of energy that can be transmitted). Some of these have shown variations with time.

If the speed of light was significantly higher when the universe was created, it could solve the problem of distant starlight and allow us to observe real events from distant space, even though the universe is young. Measurements of the speed of light over the last 300 years have shown a steady decrease of about 0.5 %, according to analysis by Barry Setterfield.[60] Obviously this is a matter of interest for creationists, but there have been people outside of the creationist camp who have decided that, for one reason or another, the speed of light must have been higher in the past than it is now.

---

[60] Setterfield & Norman, *The Atomic Constants, Light and Time*, Research Report, 1987. <www.setterfield.org/report/report.html>, March 2004.

Cosmology

In 1996, two cosmologists called Andy Albrecht and Joao Magueijo met at a conference in America and began to pursue the idea that some of the problems with the expansion of the universe could be resolved if the speed of light was slowing down. In 2000, they were featured by the BBC in a programme called *Einstein's Biggest Blunder*.[61] Einstein invented the idea of a "cosmological constant" which enables the universe to remain static, neither expanding nor contracting. The astronomers at his time believed that the stars were fixed in space, although their observations were limited by the equipment available to them. Einstein suggested that some sort of constant was needed to represent the tendency of the universe to expand in just the right amount to prevent it from collapsing in on its own gravity. However, this meant the universe had to be very finely balanced, going in neither one direction nor the other, rather like a pencil balancing on its end. He stuck with the idea for a while, then abandoned it, calling it his "biggest blunder", when Edward Hubble demonstrated that the universe was expanding. Hubble's large telescope was able to show that the light from distant galaxies was shifted to the red, so the galaxies must be moving away from us.

This gave rise to the "big bang" theory of the universe, but it didn't really solve the stability problem. A universe that comes out of a big bang cannot last for long. Either it expands too quickly or else it expands too slowly and collapses in on itself. The universe is so finely balanced that you can't tell whether or not it's going to collapse, and this condition is called "flatness". The situation is further complicated by the existence of the horizon which defines the edge of the visible universe, but does not define the whole universe. After the big bang, there is supposed to have been a rapid expansion of space called "inflation", which is not limited by the speed of light. This leaves different regions of space disconnected from each other, because the horizon from any given point is defined as the distance that light has travelled from that point. During the early days of the

---

[61] *Einstein's Biggest Blunder*, BBC Television, Channel 4 Equinox, 23 Oct. 2000, <www.setterfield.org/magueijointerview.htm>, March 2004.

universe, there would have been many visible universes, and even now, after a supposed 15 billion years, there has not been enough time for the whole universe to become connected. Even within our own visible universe, we only see as far as the horizon, and the opposite sides of the visible universe are disconnected because they are a total of 30 billion light years distant from each other. However, the visible universe does not have the appearance of being disconnected, because the background radiation is constant in every direction.

This didn't fit with the idea of rapid inflation, so Albrecht and Magueijo abandoned it and began working on a radical new idea, that the entire universe expanded within a single horizon, and to make this possible, the speed of light would have to be much higher when the universe was formed. They discovered that the variation of the speed of light didn't just resolve the horizon problem. It also resolved the flatness problem because it gave the universe a built-in thermostat, creating and destroying energy as required to keep the universe in balance. Space is not just an empty vacuum. It has an energy density called Lambda (λ) which has the property of gravity in reverse, pushing the universe apart instead of pulling it together.

Effectively they had re-invented Einstein's cosmological constant, in a way that connects the variation in the speed of light with the origin of the universe. In that case, the cosmological constant was not a blunder after all. Einstein was right all the time, except that he didn't realise the speed of light has been slowing down.

In 1988 the British astronomer Richard Ellis became interested in the possibility that the fundamental constants of the universe could change. He observed quasars, which are galaxies in the process of formation, in the far distant regions of the universe. He found that as light from the quasars passes through gas clouds, the spectral interference patterns indicated that either the electrons were different or the speed of light was greater in the distant past, so there was observable evidence in support of the theories of Albrecht and Magueijo.

In 2002, the physicist Paul Davies published a paper in *Nature*,[62] suggesting that the speed of light must have slowed down to satisfy some of the properties of black holes. I won't get into the details here, but for those who want to pursue the subject, there is a discussion article by Carl Wieland.[63]

Relativity and Time Dilation

Before the days of Einstein, people used to think that space was just an empty vacuum in which we can measure distances in the three spatial co-ordinates, length, width and height. Time was considered to be just a method of measuring the intervals between successive events. Space and time were not considered to be any kind of substance with physical properties, but all that changed when Einstein produced his theory of relativity.

In 1905 he came up with his Special Theory of Relativity, which describes some strange distortions that occur when objects move at high velocity.

- Time, measured by a clock on the moving object, slows down.
- The length of the object becomes shorter in the direction of motion.
- The mass of the object increases to satisfy energy considerations.

All these properties reach a limiting value as the velocity approaches the speed of light, so that time stops, the length of the object becomes zero, and the mass becomes infinite. The speed of light therefore defines the maximum velocity beyond which nothing can travel.

These strange phenomena occur because light always travels at the same velocity relative to an observer, regardless of how the

---

[62] Davies, P.C.W., et. al., *Black holes constrain varying constants*, Nature, 418 (6898), 8 Aug. 2002, pp. 602–603.
<www.nature.com/cgi-taf/DynaPage.taf?file=/nature/journal/v418/n6898/abs/418602a_fs.html>.
[63] Wieland, Carl, *Speed of light slowing down after all?*
<www.answersingenesis.org/docs2002/0809_cdk_davies.asp>.

observer is moving. To explain this, imagine that you are travelling down the motorway at 60mph and something overtakes you at 70mph. The vehicle will appear to overtake you at 10mph. However, if you are overtaken by a beam of light, you don't subtract your own velocity from the speed of light. It will still overtake you at the speed of light, regardless of how fast you are travelling.

Light has the special property, that it always appears the same to any observer, and the strange distortions of time, length and mass occur because objects in motion have to conform to this property.

The distortions are observed only by someone who is not moving with the object. For example, if you were standing on a railway platform watching a train go past at a velocity which is a significant proportion of the speed of light, you would see the clock on the train measuring time slowly, and the train would be shorter, and if you had a method of measuring the mass, you would find that it has increased. However, to a passenger on the train, everything on the train would appear perfectly normal. As far as he is concerned, the train is not moving. Instead the world outside is moving in the other direction and becomes distorted so that the railway platform becomes shorter, the clock on the platform slows down, and the mass of the observer on the platform increases.

In 1906, Hermann Minkowski suggested that space and time are part of the same continuum, and do not exist separately from each other. We have three-dimensional space defined by length-width and height, combined with one-dimensional time, making up four-dimensional space-time.

In 1912, Einstein realised that space-time is curved, and the curvature is influenced by gravity. He began working on his field equation, and in 1915 he completed his General Theory of Relativity, showing how space-time is distorted by matter. This included the prediction that light would be deflected by a gravitational field as it passes through curved space, and his predictions have been confirmed by astronomy.

In 1916, Karl Swarzchild produced a solution to Einstein's field equation which describes black holes, and much work has been done subsequently to describe what happens within them, and in the surrounding space. Black holes are collapsed stars that are so dense, and have such high gravitational fields, that nothing can escape from them, not even light. They are the strangest objects in space, continually sucking in matter, including whole stars, and they have a singularity at the centre, which is a point of infinite density. Time slows down in the region around a black hole, and there is a boundary called the event horizon where time stops altogether, and this represents the point of no return where anything that enters can never come out.

Some strange things happen during the approach to a black hole. Suppose a spaceship stops at a safe distance outside, so it won't get sucked in, and one of the astronauts, wearing a wristwatch, gets out and moves towards the hole. His colleagues remaining in the spaceship will see his watch slowing down as he moves toward the hole, and then when he reaches the event horizon, his watch will stop altogether. Then he will remain at the event horizon forever, because he has reached the point where time has stopped. However, we should remember that everything appears normal to an observer within his own frame of reference, so from the point of view of the astronaut, the rest of the universe is changing. As he moves toward the event horizon, he looks back at the spaceship and sees that the clock on board the ship is running faster and faster. Then he sees the stars racing around, as if the universe is rapidly growing old. He doesn't remain stranded on the event horizon as his colleagues have been led to believe. Instead he goes straight through it and gets a view of whatever is inside.

Some people have suggested that a black hole is a gateway to another universe, and if the astronaut approaches in the right direction (through one of the poles of the spinning black hole and not through the equator), he will go through the singularity and emerge from a white hole at the other end. However, this is rather speculative and nobody knows for sure.

The implications of time dilation are obvious for creationists. If time can be distorted near a black hole, to the extent that an astronaut approaching the event horizon will see the universe growing old in an instant, then it must be possible for six days in one part of the universe to correspond to billions of years elsewhere.

Starlight and Time

Russell Humphreys in his book *Starlight and Time*[64] uses relativity to show that the Earth and our solar system are young, while the rest of the universe is old.

He suggests that the universe expanded out of a black hole which became a white hole, so that matter came out, instead of falling in. The universe was originally a huge ball of water called "the deep", two light years in diameter. This is small compared with the current size of the universe but is 1000 times the diameter of our own solar system. There were no sources of light, so *"darkness was upon the face of the deep"* (Gen. 1:2). This huge mass of water collapsed in on itself, initially forming a black hole but at the same time causing nuclear fusion creating a variety of elements. The black hole exploded and became a white hole, creating large amounts of light, and as matter expanded into space the event horizon shrank. The Earth and our solar system were at the centre, inside the event horizon where time moves slowly, but as the rest of the matter passed outside the event horizon, it aged very quickly. Eventually the mass density of the universe became too small to support an event horizon, so it disappeared and we were left with the universe as we have it today, with no white hole.

Light can't travel into a white hole (it's the reverse of a black hole), but when the white hole collapsed the rest of the universe became visible from the Earth. Humphreys suggests that this occurred on the fourth day of creation and he calls it "the day when the sky opened up". The stars were formed and reached maturity, and then became visible on the Earth, in only a single day of Earth time, but in their own time they were billions of years old.

One of the assumptions of this theory is that the universe must have a boundary. If it has no boundary, then it has no centre of mass. If Earth time is different from outer-universe time, then the Earth must be at a special place in the universe called the centre. What happens at the boundary? Humphreys says that the "waters above the

---

[64] Humphreys, Russell, *Starlight and Time*, Master Books, 1994.

firmament" are still there, at the edge of space.

The work of Russell Humphreys has been criticised by experts in relativity, but has so far stood up to criticism. Furthermore, it appears to be entirely Biblical and he can quote passages from Genesis and elsewhere in support of his work.

Biblical Basis

The Biblical basis for the work of Humphreys can be summarised as follows:

- The young Earth / old universe idea seems to have some support. The Earth was created in six days, and this occurred about 6,000 years ago, but the Bible makes no claims that the universe is young. Instead it says *"To him that rideth upon the heavens of heavens, which were of old"* (Psalm 68:33).

- *"Praise ye the Lord. Praise ye the Lord from the heavens: praise him in the heights. Praise ye him, all his angels: praise ye him, all his hosts. Praise ye him, sun and moon: praise him, all ye stars of light. Praise him, ye heavens of heavens, **and ye waters that be above the heavens.**"* (Psalm 148:1-4). On this basis, the heavens are outer space, because they contain the sun, moon and stars, and the waters above the heavens are still there. Also we should note that if the Hebrew of Genesis 1:20 is understood correctly, the birds do not fly in the heavens, they fly in the *face* of the heavens, which is the atmosphere.

- There are many verses that say the heavens have expanded. Here are just a few:
  - *"Which alone spreadeth out the heavens"* (Job 9:8).
  - *"who stretchest out the heavens like a curtain"* (Psalm 104:2).
  - *"the Lord, which stretcheth forth the heavens"* (Zech. 12:1).

Humphreys goes on to quote many more verses, in fact he goes through his entire theory, quoting verses from the Bible to support his interpretation of the first four days of creation.

The Solar System

There is no simple theory for the origin of the solar system in which we live. The most popular theory is that it condensed out of a rotating nebular disk of gas and dust. The central hub of the disk condensed to form the Sun, which became compressed and heated to the point where hydrogen atoms collided and nuclear fusion began to occur. The remaining material formed the planets. In the outer region of the nebular disk, the solid matter consisted mostly of ices,[65] but in the inner region, close to the Sun, the ices evaporated, leaving behind solid grains of rock. In both regions, the grains began to stick together, forming lumps of rock near the sun and frozen snowballs further out. These are known as *planetesimals*, of varying size, but typically about a mile across. The larger planetesimals swept up the smaller ones, eventually forming the planets. However, this theory has a number of problems:

- The angular momentum of the planets in their orbit around the Sun is much higher than the angular momentum of rotation of the Sun itself. If the Sun was formed from a rotating cloud of matter that was drawn towards the centre, it should be spinning rapidly, just as an ice skater speeds up when he draws his arms inwards. The Sun is by far the largest object in the Solar System, containing more than 99% of the total mass, yet it has only 2% of the angular momentum.

- Uranus, the seventh planet from the Sun, is tilted at 98 degrees so that its equator is almost perpendicular to the plane of the ecliptic (the plane in which the planets orbit around the Sun). Instead of spinning like a top, it rolls over on its side. This is thought to be a consequence of a collision from a passing object, but a collision of such magnitude would have affected the orbit of Uranus, not just its tilt. In fact Uranus has a very circular orbit, in the plane of the ecliptic, and appears undisturbed. To

---

[65] Astronomers use the term *ices* to refer to water, methane, and ammonia which is normally solid in the outer regions of the solar system.

make matters worse, Uranus has a system of rings and moons which orbit around its equator, so these are also approximately perpendicular to the ecliptic. Such a system could not have been formed from the nebular gas cloud, and it cannot be adequately explained from the effect of collisions.

- Uranus should be expected to give off heat into space, in excess of the heat that it receives from the Sun. The other three gas giants, Jupiter, Saturn and Neptune all give off excess heat, so Uranus should be the same. In particular, it should be the same as Neptune which is similar in size, atmospheric composition, period of rotation, and exists alongside it as the next planet in the solar system. Neptune gives off more than twice the energy it receives from the Sun, but it is doubtful that Uranus gives off any excess heat at all.

- Venus, the second planet from the Sun, rotates in the opposite direction from the other planets, in *retrograde* motion rather than *prograde* (although Uranus could be considered either prograde or retrograde depending on which of the poles is considered to be North). The nebular theory predicts that all planets should rotate in the same direction, in prograde motion.

In addition to the nebular theory, there has also been the tidal theory which suggested that a large star passed by the Sun and pulled out a cigar-shaped filament of gas which condensed into planets. However, this theory didn't last long because it meant that all the planets should have the same composition as the Sun, and they do not. In particular, the planets contain lithium in proportions that correspond to the gases of inter-stellar space, but in different proportions from the Sun where nuclear reactions destroy lithium.

Age of the Earth

The nebular theory suggests that the Earth was formed by the clustering together of planetesimals. Each new planetesimal smashed into the Earth with great force, generating heat and melting the interior, during a period known as the Great Bombardment. There are various theories about how long this lasted, and it is thought to be somewhere between 100,000 and 100 million years. As the Earth heated up, a process called "differentiation" occurred, so that the metals sank to the core and the lighter materials remained in the mantle above it. At the surface, there was the solid crust, although it was continually being battered and broken up by new collisions.

As the Great Bombardment came to an end, the Earth began to settle down and the magma near the surface slowly solidified to form a more stable crust of igneous rock. The term *igneous* comes from the same Latin root that gives us the word *ignition*. It means "fire formed", and it refers to any rock that was solidified from the molten state.

Igneous rocks can be intrusive, meaning that they form below the Earth's surface, or extrusive, meaning they form at the surface by volcanic activity. The crystalline structure of the rocks depends on the rate of cooling of the magma. Intrusive rocks below the surface can take thousands of years to cool (and some would say millions or even billions of years) and they form large crystals. Extrusive rocks from volcanoes cool much more quickly and form small crystals.

Intrusive rocks can exist on the surface if they have been pushed upwards and exposed. You determine the type of rock from its structure, not necessarily from its location.

Granite is a coarse grained igneous rock consisting of quartz, mica and feldspar, and it forms slowly beneath the surface.

Now here is a surprise. Within the crystalline structure of granite, there are small radiohalos, made up of concentric rings that can be seen under a microscope. They are formed from a radioactive substance called polonium that has a short half-life. There are three isotopes with half-lives as follows:

- Polonium^{210}, 138.4 days
- Polonium^{214}, 164 microseconds
- Polonium^{218}, 3 minutes.

The halos are formed by alpha (α) particles that travel a certain distance and discolour the rock. However, the halos can only become trapped in the rock while it is solidifying, and it has to solidify quickly, otherwise all the polonium will be gone.

It's rather like a tablet that dissolves in water and forms bubbles. You drop the tablet into a glass of water and the bubbles will rise to the surface as long as the tablet is still there. If you wait until the tablet has dissolved, the bubbles will disappear, but if you freeze the water quickly while the bubbles are rising, they will be permanently trapped in the ice. The same principle applies to polonium halos. The magma has to solidify while the polonium is still there.

Even the most conservative estimates say that granite takes thousands of years to form, but the presence of polonium halos tells us something quite different, that it formed in minutes. Robert Gentry researched this subject and published his results in 1986, in his book *Creation's Tiny Mystery*.[66] It has been criticised on the grounds that uranium might have found its way into the rocks and released polonium as a transient decay product, but this has been refuted by Andrew Snelling,[67] on the basis that the proportions of polonium isotopes are incompatible with uranium decay.

Is it possible that at the time of creation, something unusual must have happened, so that a process that normally requires thousands of years was completed in a few minutes?

Geological timescales normally extend to millions of years, even though only a few thousand years might be needed for the formation of a particular type of rock. Nobody knows for sure how long it takes to form coarse-grained granite, because nobody has the time to sit and watch it happen. The age of the Earth is currently estimated at 4.5 billion years, but this is primarily based on the time required for the evolution of life.

---

[66] Gentry, R.V., *Creation's Tiny Mystery*, Earth Science Associates, 1986. See also: Helder, M., *It's About Time*, AIG, Creation 10(2)1988, pp.10-12. <www.answersingenesis.org/home/area/magazines/docs/v10n2_time.asp>, March 2004.

[67] Snelling, A.A., *Polonium Radiohalos: Still "A Very Tiny Mystery"*, ICR Impact Paper 326, August 2000, <www.icr.org/pubs/imp/imp-326.htm>, March 2004.

However, there are a number of reasons why the Earth must be younger:

- The time required for the Earth to cool to its present state, assuming that it was initially molten, is only a few thousand years if convective effects from the release of water are taken into account.[68]

- The amount of helium accumulated in the atmosphere, as a consequence of radioactive decay of uranium, thorium and other elements in the rocks, suggests that the Earth is a maximum of two million years old. However, if the amount of helium remaining in the rocks is taken into account, then the age reduces to a few thousand years.[69]

- The rate of decay of the Earth's magnetic field suggests that the Earth cannot be more than about 10,000 years old.[70]

Appearance of Age

We have seen how the presence of polonium halos in granite suggests the rapid formation of rock which, from all other accounts, has the appearance of greater age (although not the billions of years suggested by evolutionists). The appearance of age is actually a Biblical concept, for example Adam and Eve were created as mature adults, not as infants. The fruit that they ate was from mature trees that were created only three days earlier, including the tree of knowledge of good and evil that brought their downfall.

Even in the New Testament, we see things created with the appearance of age. The Gospel of John is sometimes referred to as

---

[68] Snelling, A.A., Woodmorappe, J., *Rapid Rocks*, AIG, Creation 21(1) Dec. 1998–Feb. 1999, pp. 42–44, <www.answersingenesis.org/docs/3970.asp>, March 2004.

[69] Sarfati, J.D., *Blowing Old-Earth Belief Away*, AIG, Creation 20(3)1998, pp.19–21, <www.answersingenesis.org/docs/1401.asp>, March 2004.

[70] Sarfati, J.D., *The Earth's Magnetic Field: Evidence that the Earth is Young*, AIG, Creation 20(2)1998, pp.15-17, <www.answersingenesis.org/creation/v20/i2/magnetic.asp>, March 2004.

the "Creation Gospel", because it contains many passages that relate to creation in some way. In particular, the first chapter starts with *"In the beginning was the Word"*, then it compares light and darkness, then it goes on to talk about the true Light and the witness to the Light, comparing Jesus and John the Baptist to the Sun and Moon.

In chapter two we have the marriage in Cana in Galilee, where there are six pots of water, representing the six days of creation. Jesus turns it into wine, and it turns out to be better than the wine that they have drunk already. The question is, how long does it take to make good wine? It needs to be stored for months or even years, until it becomes fully mature, but Jesus was able to make good wine instantly. The purpose of this miracle was to demonstrate that he was the creator of the world, and he could create things with the appearance of age.

The appearance of age is just a normal feature of creation and there is nothing strange about it. God creates things in whatever physical state is required, including states of maturity that imply an apparent age.

The appearance of age should not be confused with time dilation, which is the passage of actual time according to a local clock. The universe runs at different rates according to the properties of space-time, but it nevertheless represents real time.

Also, the appearance of age does not imply an apparent history, and should not be confused with the notion of the creation of light in transit. We have already mentioned that light travelling through space contains information about events that happened in the past, and therefore the simultaneous creation of stars and starlight would be deceptive. The creation of the world with an apparent age does not have this problem. It implies an age, but it does not display a history, even though cosmologists might look for one.

Life on Other Planets

This is something that everybody wonders about. Here we are, on this tiny planet, in a vast universe where there must be many other similar planets. We know there are planets around some of the stars, because we can see the stars wobbling as the planets orbit around them. We normally think of planets orbiting stars, but in reality, the planet and star orbit around each other, with a centre of gravity close to the larger body, which is the star. The bigger the planet, the more it will cause the star to wobble, and the planets that cause an observable effect on the stars in the sky are more likely to be gas giants like Jupiter, rather than small planets like Earth. Nevertheless, it is very reasonable to believe that a few planets, just like the Earth, exist somewhere in space, with an environment that is capable of supporting life. The question is, should we expect to find life on such a planet?

Evolutionists believe that life evolved spontaneously on our planet, without any need for God, or any act of creation. Evolution should therefore be expected to occur on any other planet where the same conditions exist, and the search for alien life forms is considered to be a high priority.

Some creationists believe that there is no life in space, except for the life that is here on Earth. The Bible says nothing about life on other planets, so why should we expect it to exist? Would God create other life forms, on other planets, and not tell us anything about them? What should we do if we meet an alien? Why has God not given us any instructions about what to say to them? Are they capable of knowing the difference between good and evil, and are they in need of salvation?

I would say that the reason why we have no instructions about aliens is because we don't need any. If God has created aliens, on another planet, and if somehow they have gained the knowledge of good and evil, God will deal with them in his own way. The Bible is for us, not for aliens. Jesus came as a man, to give salvation to humanity. If he wanted to save aliens, he would have gone as an alien, to their planet. What would I do if I met an alien? I would probably ask him "What sort of Bible have you got?", although I would be concerned that he might be like Adam, in his unfallen state, and I would not want to be the one who teaches him the difference between good and evil.

Anyway, putting aside the spiritual implications, how can we detect the presence of aliens in the universe? There are only three ways, either we have to go there, or they have to come here, or we communicate by radio and other signals from the sky. It's impractical to travel between the stars, because of the great distances, but the aliens might be able to come here if they have some kind of technology that's more advanced than ours. Some people have thought that UFO's are aliens from outer space, while others think they are fallen angels from a demonic realm, attempting to repeat the events of Genesis 6 when the *sons of God* cohabited with the *daughters of men*.[71]

Nobody seems to know what to do about UFO's (or perhaps somebody knows and they won't tell us), so the only practical efforts we can make are to send out radio signals into space and listen to what comes back. However, the distances are measured in light years, so if we want to say something, and it gets picked up by somebody out there, we won't get a reply until years later. However, we can hope that somebody out there is also sending out signals, waiting for us to respond, but where are they, and what frequency are they using? We don't know, but it's a reasonable assumption that they will send out a signal at about 1420 MHz, corresponding to the spectral frequency of hydrogen which is the most abundant substance in space. This is a quiet frequency that is relatively free from noise and therefore most suitable for radio transmissions. It is also likely that they will concentrate their signal into a narrow bandwidth for greater efficiency, and this will distinguish it from naturally occurring radio waves which are distributed over a relatively wide bandwidth. The signal might also be pulsed, if the aliens have decided that this will make it more distinct. If it is transmitted from a planet, there might be a slight change in frequency due to the doppler effect of the planet's movement and rotation, just as the siren of a police car drops in frequency as it goes past you in the street. A signal from an alien source will be weak compared with naturally occurring radio waves, but if the data from radio telescopes is analysed carefully enough, it might be possible to

---

[71] Missler, C., Eastman, M., *Alien Encounters*, Koinonia House, <www.khouse.org/conferences/alien/>.

find a few signals with the right characteristics, arising from specific points in space, giving possible evidence of alien activity.

Since the late 1950's, various projects have been undertaken to search the sky using radio telescopes, and the computers required to analyse the large amount of data have become gradually more sophisticated. These efforts have become generically known as SETI (Search for Extra-Terrestrial Intelligence).

A lot of computing power is required to analyse the data, placing a heavy load even on the most powerful super-computers, but a novel approach is being used by the SETI@home project based in Berkeley, California.[72] They break up the data into small packets and send it to home computer users all over the world, using the internet, for analysis by a screen saver program that runs automatically when the computer is not being used for other purposes. When a signal is discovered that looks interesting, the user is alerted, although this doesn't necessarily mean that it's time to celebrate the discovery of alien life forms. First a report has to be sent back to the project team and they will perform additional tests. If they think that it could be a genuine alien source, they will make a public announcement so that astronomers all over the world can start looking at the appropriate section of the sky.

There are a few million computer users involved in the SETI@home project, but in spite of this and various other projects that have been undertaken during a period of more than four decades, nobody has received a signal that genuinely appears to represent alien activity. If it happened, it would be big news.

The question is, why is it so difficult to find life in space, after all the effort that has been made? The reason, probably, is because there is nobody out there. For evolutionists, this might seem unthinkable, and they would even consider it to be a position of arrogance, that we are the only intelligent beings in the whole universe. For creationists, it shouldn't really matter one way or the

---

[72] SETI@home, University of California, Berkeley,
<http://setiathome.ssl.berkeley.edu/>.
See also: SETI, <http://seti.ssl.berkeley.edu/>.

other. We don't need to find alien life, just to prove that our view of the universe is correct, but if we find somebody out there, we would be equally curious to know who they are and what they are doing.

In the Beginning

This Appendix has gone briefly through a lot of issues related to the cosmos, and it seems appropriate at this point to look at the first verse of the Bible because it appears to be saying something that might be relevant to the strange distortions of space and time that we have already discussed.

> In the beginning God created the heaven and the earth.

This verse represents three components of the universe:

- *In the beginning* represents time.

- *Heaven* represents space.

- *Earth* represents matter.

To the casual reader, the phrase *"In the beginning"* appears to be just the starting point for the creation narrative. However, since it appears alongside *"heaven"*, we cannot avoid the implication that it represents part of the creation itself. Space and time are part of the same continuum, known as four-dimensional space-time, and they do not exist separately from each other. Space-time is a substance with physical properties, not just a vague abstraction, and therefore it has to be created.

The appearance of matter alongside space-time is highly significant, because it means we have all the components that make up Einstein's General Theory of Relativity. We have seen how matter, which has the property of gravity, defines the curvature of space-time. Energy is notably missing because it is interchangeable with matter, but without it you would have a dead universe. This is significant because in verse 2 we have *"darkness was upon the face of the deep"*. Then in verse 3 we have *"Let there be light"* which could mean the conversion of some of the matter into energy, and we already have the space-time through which light can propagate. Then in verses 4 and 5 we have the separation of light from darkness, which is probably a general statement about properties that are capable of variation. This brings us to the end of the first day of creation, and we see that it describes the physical laws of the universe, and not just the universe itself.

This makes sense because the universe would not be meaningful without any physical laws. The laws were defined on the first day, and then the rest of the creation could continue.

When we consider that space-time is part of the creation, and we see it doing some very strange things in an apparently mature universe, how can we possibly imagine what it was doing when the universe was created? We hesitate even to use the word "when" because such a concept implies the existence of time. Was the universe created in six days or billions of years, and what sort of clock was used to measure time in each part of the cosmos? None of us are in a position to answer such a question, because we were not there at the "time".

Then the Lord answered Job out of the whirlwind, and said, ...Where wast thou when I laid the foundations of the earth? Declare, if thou hast understanding.

Job 38:1-4

184

Appendix 5 - Creation Science Resources

There are so many books and audio-visual materials on creation science that it would be impossible to list them all here, and in any case the list would soon become out of date as new resources become available. It would be equally pointless attempting to list all the organisations that support creation science in some way. While writing this Appendix, I looked at the Google[73] search engine and typed in "creation science" and got more than 60,000 results. Looking at just a small sample of these I found that it included both supporters and opponents of creation science, and some organisations that don't take any view one way or the other, and many books and other resources.

Rather than attempt a comprehensive list, I will just mention a few organisations that stand out as major suppliers of creation resources.

- **Creation Science Movement.** This organisation is based in the UK and is the oldest creationist organisation in the world, having started off in 1932 as the "Evolution Protest Movement". They send a newsletter to members every two months, together with a pamphlet covering some specific aspect of creation research. In 2000 they opened the "Genesis Expo", a permanent exhibition on the harbour front at Portsmouth, close to the historic ships which attract many tourists. Contact: CSM, PO Box 888, Portsmouth, PO6 2YD, UK. <www.csm.org.uk>.

- **Answers in Genesis.** This is the largest creationist organisation, with its headquarters in Australia and offices in the UK, USA, Canada, South Africa and New Zealand. They produce a quarterly magazine called *Creation*, and for those who want to

---

[73] Google search engine <www.google.com>.

185

go into the issues in greater depth, they have the *Technical Journal* (normally abbreviated *TJ*). This is a peer-reviewed journal that gives creationists the opportunity to publish their research, an opportunity that is normally denied to them in other journals. You don't need to have any special qualifications to publish something. All you need is a well reasoned argument, and you have to follow the *Instructions to Authors* which appear at the end of each issue. Contact: AIG, PO Box 6302, Acacia Ridge, QLD 4110, Australia. <www.AnswersInGenesis.org>. International addresses are available from the website.

- **Institute for Creation Research.** This is the largest creationist research organisation in the USA, supported by many highly qualified scientists in a wide range of fields. They produce a monthly newsletter *Arts & Facts*, including *Impact* articles discussing specific issues, mostly scientific, and *Back to Genesis* articles, discussing theological issues and other matters of importance to Christians. The *Impact* and *Back to Genesis* articles are available from their website, separately from *Arts & Facts*. Contact: The Museum of Creation and Earth History, ICR Graduate School, 10946 Woodside Ave. North, Santee, CA 92071, USA. <www.icr.org>.

All the above organisations have a catalogue of books and other resources which is regularly updated. They also have online stores so you can buy their materials through the Internet.

There are many other creationist books, not listed by any of these organisations, and they should not be considered sub-standard or inferior just because they are not listed. The inclusion of a book in a catalogue is based on marketing and other considerations, and sometimes a book will be excluded because, for some reason, it does not support the aims and objectives of the organisation, or it might get into speculative issues that would draw the organisation into arguments that they cannot resolve. Sometimes, an organisation will exclude a book from their own catalogue, but they will still recommend it as a useful resource and will encourage you to buy it from elsewhere.

There is a growing industry of self-published authors who are using small-volume digital printing, and making their books available through their own Internet shopping carts, and from major online distributors such as Amazon, Barnes & Noble, Blackwell, etc. It's relatively easy to get a book distributed by one of these organisations, because they have a policy of selling everything, while keeping hardly anything on the shelves.

On the evolutionist side, I would recommend *The Origin of Species*, by Charles Darwin (see Bibliography). This is the classic work that started off the evolution debate, but the reader will find that Darwin's views are very moderate compared with today's evolutionists. He discusses the question of variation and natural selection, which most creationists would agree with, and then he discusses the question of major transitions as a possibility but not a certainty.

I wouldn't recommend any modern evolutionist books, because there is a concerted campaign to stifle debate rather than to encourage it. For example, some evolutionists, including some book authors, are trying to get the creation and evolution debate removed from the school curriculum in the UK.[74]

There are a number of Internet forums where you can discuss creation and evolution, but the standard of debate leaves much to be

---

[74] **England and Wales:** National Curriculum, Key Stage 4, Science, SC1 Scientific Enquiry. Ideas and evidence in science. (1) Pupils should be taught: ... (b) how scientific controversies can arise from different ways of interpreting empirical evidence [for example, Darwin's theory of evolution]. <www.nc.uk.net/nc/contents/Sc-4-1-POS.html>.
Scotland: 5-14 National Guidelines, (2) Framework for Environmental Studies, (2.6) Developing informed attitudes: ... Through their learning in social subjects, science and technology, pupils will begin to appreciate differences in ways of thinking, working and viewing the world. <www.ltscotland.org.uk/5to14/htmlguidelines/environmental/page15.htm>.
Northern Ireland: Curriculum: Key Stage 4 Science: The Nature of Science: Pupils ... should study examples of scientific controversies and the ways in which scientific ideas developed. <www.deni.gov.uk/parents/key_stages/pdfs/science/4_scie_sgl.pdf>.

desired. The Internet as a whole suffers from a problem called "flaming", which means pouring out abuse against people you have never met, from the safety and isolation of your own home or office. This problem is especially persistent in creation/evolution forums, where evolutionists pour out personal abuse against creationists, saying things they would never say if they met them face to face. The most popular trick is to try and find something that they think is a fault in a creationist argument, and then accuse the person of telling lies. The approach is something like this: "I'm right and you are wrong. But you knew that, didn't you? But you didn't say so, did you? So you are a liar". To make matters worse, you can't even find out who is calling you a liar, because they don't use their real names, they use aliases. Most creationists won't put up with this for long, so they disappear from the forums, leaving the evolutionists to talk to each other.

To avoid the problem of flaming, some creationists have set up their own forums which are carefully moderated. All participants are asked to agree to a set of rules, and anyone who breaks them is thrown out. In these forums, you can discuss your theories in peace, without being subjected to personal attacks.

There are many forums, both open and moderated, that discuss the creation/evolution issue in some way, but they tend to be transient because they depend on regular participation from people who are willing to observe the rules and stay on track. Rather than trying to recommend something specific, I would suggest that you go to one of the major suppliers of Internet forums, such as Yahoo Groups[75] and search for "creation science". Then you can choose whatever suits you best, from the list that comes up.

There are, of course, many opportunities to discuss the issues locally, by talking to people face to face. If you want to find people who understand the scientific issues, and are not just carrying philosophical baggage, probably the best resource is the local education system. There are many schoolteachers who are very open minded and have accumulated knowledge and experience by having

---

[75] Yahoo Groups <groups.yahoo.com>.

to explain the issues in different types of class situation. Many of them would welcome the opportunity to discuss the issues outside the constraints of the education system. However, teachers are busy people and might not have the time. If this is the case, it might be best to try and find someone who is retired.

Appendix 6 - Creation History

When Charles Darwin's *Origin of Species* was first published in 1859, it started off a heated debate between people of various persuasions, both scientific and theological, about whether or not life could come into existence of its own accord without the intervention of a Creator. Darwin had spent many years collecting specimens and researching the possible causes of change, and came up with the idea that small changes could occur because of the exposure of a species to its environment, a process that he called "natural selection". Then he suggested that, over a long period of time, small changes would accumulate into big changes, so that higher life forms could evolve from those that were most primitive. He was soon followed by Thomas Huxley, a medical doctor and accomplished biologist, who suggested that humans had descended from ape-like creatures. He is best known for his debate with Samuel Wilberforce, Bishop of Oxford, in 1860, in which Wilberforce is alleged to have asked Huxley if he had descended from an ape on his grandmother's side or his grandfather's side. Huxley responded to this by giving a spirited scientific defence of evolution, concluding with the remark that he would rather be descended from an ape than a bishop.

There are different accounts of the Huxley-Wilberforce debate, but most accounts agree that Huxley won the day because of his superior skill in science. This event has become part of evolution folklore, but it was characteristic of the time, because generally, the opponents of evolution were theologians who were more familiar with Biblical interpretation and relatively unskilled in science.

In the process of time, evolution began to take its place as scientific orthodoxy, and opposition to the theory was considered to be religion rather than science. The debate became polarised along scientific/religious lines, creating the myth that still persists today, that you can't be a "real" scientist if you don't believe in evolution. This is clearly an unsatisfactory situation for anyone trying to do objective research. There were some scientists who objected to being put in an ideological straight-jacket, and in 1932 they formed the "Evolution Protest Movement", which subsequently became the "Creation Science Movement" that I have mentioned in Appendix 5.

This was followed by the formation of other creationist movements around the world, able to present sophisticated arguments against evolution, from many branches of science.

However, the emphasis on science has left an important area of research relatively unexplored. If the world was created in a short period of time, just a few thousand years ago, and all humans and air-breathing animals were subsequently destroyed in a global flood, except for those that were saved in the ark, then we should expect to have a continuous history of the world, from that time up to the present. Indeed we do, and the most comprehensive early history is in the Bible, but because of the polarisation of the creation/evolution debate, and hostility towards anything that has the appearance of religion, the Bible is denounced as a book of myths that are not to be taken seriously. To persuade people that these events, as recorded in the Bible, are historic facts, we have to appeal to other sources and show that they match up with the Bible. This includes sources that describe creation, the flood, the dispersion from Babylon, the journey of Abraham to Canaan, the captivity of the Israelites in Egypt and their eventual departure at the time of Moses, and the continuing history of Israel.

Before the time of Darwin, many history books, if not most of them, started with a few lines about creation, the flood, and the dispersion of the three sons of Noah to different parts of the world. For example, there is the poetic verse of *Albions England*, by William Warner, containing the following lines:[76]

> When Arked Noah, and few with him,
> the emptied worlds remain,
> Had left the instrumental means,
> of landing them again,
> And that both man and beast, and all,
> did multiply the store,
> To Asia Shem, to Affrick Ham,
> to Europe Japheth bore.

---

[76] Warner, William, *Albions England*, first published in 1586. I have slightly modernised these lines to make them more readable.

Also we have John of Fordun's *Chronicle of the Scottish Nation* which has the following lines:[77]

> Almighty God, the Creator and Ruler of all things, willed in his Creation, according to the philosophers, that the World should be round, and in its mid-most region He placed the Earth, the mother, nurse, and abode of all animate, material, and rational things; separated, as a central point, from all parts of the heavens by an equal interval.
> ...
> The sons of Noah shared the world among themselves, after the Flood, in the following manner:- Shem, with his descendants, took possession of Asia, Japhet, of Europe, and Ham, of Africa. From them was the whole human race distributed in nations and kingdoms over the earth.

Note that John of Fordun, who lived from about 1320 to 1385, gave a pre-Copernican view of the Earth at the centre of the universe, although he attributed this to the philosophers (probably the Greeks), as if he was aware that it doesn't come from the Bible.

In those days, theologians used to quote liberally from sources outside the Bible, including the philosophies and mythologies of other nations. Most histories were written by the clergy, who were among the few people who knew how to read and write. After beginning their histories with a few lines about creation and the flood, they would invariably move on to tales from Egyptian and Greek mythology, which appear to bear some relation to events in the Bible, and then they would gradually proceed to the histories of their own time.

The careful reader, who takes the time to investigate the sources of these mythological tales, will find that they do exist, and were written long before the Christian era, by people who had never seen a Bible. For example, Homer, who lived in the eighth century BC,

---

[77] Skene, W.F., *John of Fordun: Chronicle of the Scottish Nation*, pp.1,3.

tells us how Poseidon (Neptune) spoke to his brothers as follows:[78]

> We are three brothers, sons of Cronos, born from Rhea-Zeus, myself,
> and Hades, third brother, ruler of the dead. The whole world was
> divided in three parts, and each of us received one share. Once the lots
> were shaken, I won the blue-gray sea as mine to live in for ever. Hades
> got the gloomy darkness, Zeus wide heaven, with upper air and clouds.
> But earth and high Olympus still remained common to all of us.

Clearly, the three brothers are styled on Shem, Ham and Japheth, but
instead of being given three parts of the earth, they have the sea, sky
and the world below, with the earth in common. I have already
mentioned, in Appendix 1, how the confinement of Osiris is styled
on Noah entering the Ark, and there are many other examples from
different parts of the world, showing how the most ancient histories
are remembered by the nations, wherever they have been scattered.

I will not attempt to describe all of these here, but there is plenty
of evidence to show that, from a creationist point of view, there is
much to be gained from history as well as science. The
creation/evolution debate, since the time of Darwin, has been almost
entirely focused on science, to the point that, for the casual
participant, it would appear as if nobody has bothered to look at the
records left behind by our ancestors. I have already mentioned some
of the limitations of science in Appendix 1, that scientific
observation is subject to multiple interpretations, and it can find out
about the past only by extrapolation from the present, and becomes
more and more unreliable as you go further back. I will now add a
further difficulty, that science can only tell us about the conditions
that might have existed in the past, not about the actual events. To
illustrate the point, the investigation of a crime can only begin when
someone reports that the crime has actually occurred. The person
who reports the crime has to be either a victim, or a witness, or
someone who has heard about it from a third party. There has to be a

---

[78] Homer, *The Iliad*, XV, 187-192. Translated by Ian Johnston, Malaspina
University-College, Nanaimo, British Columbia. <www.mala.bc.ca/
~johnstoi/homer/iliad15.htm>. See also Rieu, E.V.

historical report of the crime, from some source or other. There would be no point using forensic science, or other methods of investigation, for a crime that never occurred. Even after the crime has been reported, there might be a need for other historical evidence to resolve it. For example, if a dead body is dug up, in a state of decay, it might be necessary to identify the body from dental records. But to have dental records, there needs to be a history of visits to the dentist.

Applying the same principles to historical work, you might dig up a body with a long, narrow hole in the skull, and decide that the person must have been hit with an axe, but you need historical records to find out in which battle he fought, and who was his king.

The problem with Darwinian evolution is that they try to investigate events that are supposed to have occurred in the distant past, millions of years ago, before there was any recorded history. They are taking science beyond its limits, giving a distinct advantage to creationists who are able to combine both science and history in their favour. Alongside creation science, we have another supporting discipline called *creation history*.

Most creationists today recognise the value of historical research, although the number of people who get actively involved is small compared with those who are involved with science. This is a reflection of society as a whole, where science and technology are considered to be of primary importance for economic progress, and history is considered to be of lesser importance, because it's "all in the past" and you can't do much with it. Of course we can tell people that we need history to understand ourselves and the society we live in, but that's not much of an inspiration for young graduates who are looking for jobs.

Even among those who are actively involved in creation history research, there are many people who have more formal training in science than in history. That's not such a bad thing, because whenever somebody gives a talk on ancient history, going back to creation and the flood, and they say "Any questions?", they always get asked science questions. This can be quite intimidating for a historian who does not have a scientific background, and it's probably the reason why very few of them are willing to get involved. However, historians are definitely needed, to keep the scientists on the right track, and to get involved in the translation and preservation of ancient documents.

Creation History Resources

There are a number of people around the world who are doing research into creation history, and writing books and articles, but for the most part, they don't try to set up their own organisations. Instead they participate in organisations that have already been set up to support creation science, or creationism more generally. The three major creationist organisations, CSM, AIG and ICR, already mentioned in Appendix 5, all take an interest in creation history and have published numerous articles in their journals and magazines. If you ask them about any aspect of historical research, they will usually be able to point you in the right direction, and will recommend books and other resources from their own catalogue and elsewhere.

My first book, *Forgotten History of the Western People*,[79] gives a panoramic view of history, starting with creation and the flood from Babylonian sources, which bear a striking similarity to the Bible, although there are differences of detail. It continues with the hierarchies of the Greek and Egyptian gods, and the claims of Euhemerus that all the gods are deified kings. Then it continues with the foundation of Troy and its eventual destruction, and the flight of Aeneas to Italy where he set up his new kingdom. His great-grandson Brutus came to Britain, and was the first of a long line of kings who enjoyed independence until they were invaded by the Romans and were obliged to coexist with them as vassal kings. Then the Romans left, creating a political vacuum that was filled by the Saxons who drove the Britons into Wales. There is also a discussion of the Scottish and Irish histories, and the arrival of Christianity in

---

[79] Gascoigne, Mike, *Forgotten History of the Western People: From the Earliest Origins*, Anno Mundi Books, 2002, <www.annomundi.co.uk>, March 2004.

Britain during the first century. The final chapter tells us how the world will end, from the viewpoint of pagan apocalyptic literature that bears some relation to the Bible. I have also found the following books helpful:[80]

- *After the Flood* by Bill Cooper. This book shows how the early pagans knew about the true God, because of their descent from Noah, and there is a history of the descendants of Japheth that make up the European nations. There is also a table of nations giving the Biblical descendants of all three sons of Noah, and the nations that have sprung from them. This book was the main inspiration that got me started on the study of Creation History.

- *The Genesis Record* by Henry Morris. This is a comprehensive and detailed commentary on Genesis, from a creationist viewpoint. It suggests that Genesis was written by a number of different authors, and the various components were eventually put together and compiled by Moses. The authors were all participants in the story, including God who wrote the first part, about the six days of creation. Each successive author signed off with the phrase *"These are the generations of ... "*, and then wrote his name.

- *Adam and His Kin* by Ruth Beechick. This is a story book, very easy to read, based on the first few chapters of Genesis from creation until the departure of Abraham from Ur of the Chaldees. It includes some fictional events and dialogues which are all very feasible, enhancing the story without distracting from the recorded Biblical history.

- *Genesis: Finding Our Roots*, also by Ruth Beechick. This follows the same theme as *Adam and His Kin*, but it's much more of a homeschooling resource with lesson notes and suggestions for further study. It's a well illustrated hardback book, comparing Biblical themes with classical art and literature, and is intended to be used together with *Adam and His Kin* and *The Genesis Record*.

---

[80] See Bibliography.

The above books have all been written in recent times to address current needs, but they stand on the shoulders of their predecessors, as this book does, and they have bibliographies for the benefit of those who want to go deeper.

Bibliography

*Dates appearing after Web pages
indicate when they were last accessed.*

Apollodorus, (2nd century BC) - see Frazer, Sir James George.

Aristotle, (384-322 BC) - see Tredennick, Hugh.

Atkins, Peter, *The Elements of Physical Chemistry*, Oxford, 2001.

Babbitt, Frank Cole, *Plutarch: Moralia,* Vol. V, Loeb Classical Library, 1936. <www.ukans.edu/history/index/europe/ ancient_rome/E/Roman/Texts/Plutarch/Moralia/ Isis_and_Osiris*/home.html>, March 2004.

Beechick, Ruth, *Adam And His Kin*, Mott Media, 1991.

Beechick, Ruth, *Genesis: Finding Our Roots*, Arrow Press, 1997.

Bivin, David; Blizzard, Roy B., *Understanding the Difficult Words of Jesus: New Insights from a Hebraic Perspective*, Destiny Image, 1995.

Bryant, Jacob, *A New System or an Analysis of Ancient Mythology*, 6 volumes, first published 1774. Third edition 1807, London: Printed for J. Walker & others. Facsimile reprint of 1774 edition, vols. 1-3, from Kessinger Publishing Co., 2003.

Charles, R.H. *The Book of Enoch: Translations of Early Documents*, Society for Promoting Christian Knowledge, London, 1917.

Cooper, Bill, *After the Flood*, New Wine Press, 1995.

Cundick, Allan, *The Divine Revelation of the Future: An Expository Study of the Book of Revelation*, 2 volumes, 2001, Christian Year Publications, The Glebe House, Stanton Drew, Bristol, BS18 4EH, UK.

Bibliography

Darwin, Charles, *The Origin of Species*, with introduction and notes by Gillian Beer, Oxford University Press, 1998. First published by John Murray, London, 1859.

Davidson, F., *The New Bible Commentary*, London, Inter-Varsity Fellowship, 1954.

Davies, P.C.W., Davis, T.M., Lineweaver, C.H., *Black holes constrain varying constants*, Nature, vol. 418, no. 6898, 8 Aug. 2002, pp. 602–603. <www.nature.com/cgi-taf/DynaPage.taf?file=/nature/journal/v418/n6898/abs/418602a_fs.html>, March 2004.

Einstein's Biggest Blunder, BBC Television, Channel 4 Equinox, 23 Oct. 2000, <www.setterfield.org/magueijointerview.htm>, March 2004.

Fordun, John, (c.1320 - c.1385) - see Skene, William F.

Frazer, Sir James George (editor), *Apollodorus: The Library*, 2 Volumes. Cambridge, MA, Harvard University Press; London, William Heinemann Ltd. 1921. Volume 2 includes *Epitome*. See also: *Library and Epitome*, <www.perseus.tufts.edu/cgi-bin/ptext?lookup=Apollod.>, March 2004.

Fruchtenbaum, Arnold G., *The Footsteps of the Messiah*, 1983, Revised Edition, 2003, Ariel Ministries, PO Box 3723, Tustin, CA 92781, <www.ariel.org>, March 2004.

Fruchtenbaum, Arnold G., *The Jewish Wedding System and the Bride of Christ*, Ariel Ministries, 1983.

Gascoigne, Mike, *Forgotten History of the Western People: From the Earliest Origins*, Anno Mundi Books, 2002, <www.annomundi.co.uk>, March 2004.

Gentry, Robert V., *Creation's Tiny Mystery*, Earth Science Associates, Knoxville, TN, 1986, <www.halos.com/books.htm>, March 2004.

Hales, Roy. L., various articles in Creation Social Science and Humanities Quarterly Journal: *The Original World Monotheism*, Vol. VII, No. 2, 1984, pp. 18-21; *Mythology, The Bible and the Postflood Origins of Greek History*, Vol. VII, No. 4, 1985, pp. 20-23; <www.creationism.org/csshs/index.htm>, March 2004.

Helder, Margaret, *It's About Time*, Answers in Genesis, Creation, 10(2)1988, pp.10–12. <www.answersingenesis.org/home/area/magazines/docs/v10n2_time.asp>, March 2004.

Homer, (8th century BC) - See Johnston, Ian, and Rieu, EV.

Humphreys, Russell., *Starlight and Time*, Master Books, 1994.

Johnston, Ian, *Homer: The Iliad*, Malaspina University-College, Nanaimo, BC, Canada, <www.mala.bc.ca/~johnstoi/homer/iliad_title.htm>, March 2004.

Jowett, Benjamin, *Plato's Dialogues: Phaedo*, <www.bartleby.com/2/1/31.html>, March 2004.

Levitt, Zola, *A Christian Love Story*, 1978, Zola Levitt Ministries, PO Box 12268, Dallas, Texas 75225-0268, USA. <www.levitt.com>, March 2004.

Manuel, Frank E., *Isaac Newton: Historian*, Cambridge University Press, 1963.

Missler, C., Eastman, M., *Alien Encounters*, Koinonia House, <www.khouse.org/conferences/alien/>, March 2004.

Morris, Henry M., *Bible-Believing Scientists of the Past*, Institute for Creation Research, Impact Paper 103, January 1982. <http://www.icr.org/pubs/imp/imp-103.htm>, March 2004.

Morris, Henry M., *The Genesis Record*, Baker Book House, 1976, <www.bakerbooks.com>, March 2004.

Parada, Carlos, *Greek Mythology Link*, <homepage.mac.com/cparada/GML>, March 2004.

Bibliography

Perry, S.V., Harris, Sir H., Pickstone, J., Gall, J., *Development of the Cell Concept*, <www.discoveryofthecell.net>, March 2004.

Plato, (4th century BC) - see Jowett, Benjamin.

Plutarch (AD c.46 - c.122) - see Babbitt, Frank Cole.

Rieu, E.V., *Homer: The Iliad*, Penguin Classics, 1950.

Rogers, G.F.C., Mayhew, Y.R., *Engineering Thermodynamics: Work and Heat Transfer*, 4th Edition, 1992, Longman.

Sarfati, Jonathan D., *Blowing Old-Earth Belief Away*, Answers in Genesis, Creation, 20(3)1998, pp.19–21, <www.answersingenesis.org/docs/1401.asp>, March 2004.

Sarfati, Jonathan D., *The Earth's Magnetic Field: Evidence that the Earth is Young*, Answers in Genesis, Creation, 20(2)1998, pp.15-17, <www.answersingenesis.org/creation/v20/i2/magnetic.asp>, March 2004.

Setterfield, B., Norman, T., *The Atomic Constants, Light and Time*, Research Report, 1987, prepared for Lambert Dolphin, Senior Research Physicist at Stanford Research Institute International. <www.setterfield.org/report/report.html>, March 2004.

SETI (Search for Extra-Terrestrial Intelligence), University of California, Berkeley, <http://seti.ssl.berkeley.edu/>, Mar. 2004. See also: SETI@home, <http://setiathome.ssl.berkeley.edu/>, Mar. 2004.

Skene, William F., (translator and editor), *John of Fordun: Chronicle of the Scottish Nation.* First published in Edinburgh, 1872, as volume IV of *The Historians of Scotland.* Facsimile reprint in two volumes, 1993, Llanerch Press, Lampeter, Ceredigion.

Snelling, Andrew A., *Polonium Radiohalos: Still "A Very Tiny Mystery"*, Institute for Creation Research, Impact Paper 326, August 2000, <www.icr.org/pubs/imp/imp-326.htm>, March 2004.

Snelling, Andrew A., *Radioactive 'dating' failure*, Answers in Genesis, Creation, 22(1), Dec. 1999 - Feb. 2000, pp.18-21. <www.answersingenesis.org/home/area/magazines/docs/cenv22n1_dating_failure.asp>, March 2004.

Snelling, A.A., Woodmorappe, J., *Rapid Rocks*, Answers in Genesis, Creation, 21(1), Dec. 1998 - Feb. 1999, pp. 42-44, <www.answersingenesis.org/docs/3970.asp>, March 2004.

Tredennick, Hugh, *Aristotle: Metaphysics*, Books I-IX, Loeb Classical Library, Harvard Univ. Press, June 1979. For Book I see: <www.non-contradiction.com/ac_works_b37.asp>, March 2004.

Warner, William, *Albions England*, 1612, first published 1586. Reprinted by Anglistica & Americana, Georg Olms Verlag, Hildesheim, New York, 1971.

Wieland, Carl, *Speed of light slowing down after all?*, <www.answersingenesis.org/docs2002/0809_cdk_davies.asp>, March 2004.

World English Bible, POB 15762, Long Beach, CA, 90815, USA. <http://ebible.org>, March 2004.

Index

Printed in the United Kingdom
by Lightning Source UK Ltd.
99862UKS00001B/109-180